MEETING ANANIAS

AND OTHER EYE-OPENING STORIES OF FAITH

James Tino

TRI-PILLAR PUBLISHING

MEETING ANANIAS

Tri-Pillar Publishing
Anaheim Hills, California
Website: www.TriPillarPublishing.com
e-mail: tripillarpublishing@cox.net

International Standard Book Number --13:
    978-0-9818923-9-9

International Standard Book Number --10:
    0-9818923-9-6

Library of Congress Control Number:
    2014931048

First edition, January, 2014

Printed in the United States of America

This book is dedicated to my wife Liisa, the best missionary I have ever known, and to all of those who labored together with us in Venezuela. May we all continue to follow our Missionary God wherever He leads!

Contents

Contents *(continued)*

Acknowledgments

Someone once said that writing a book is like a dance between the author and the editor – each needs to know when to lead and when to follow; when to step forward, and when to step back. I am blessed beyond measure to have experienced my first "author's dance" with the talented and dedicated team at Tri-Pillar Publishing:

- Josephine Dibble, prayerful and passionate, enthusiastic and encouraging – you taught me how to write
- Andy Dibble, patient and watchful, measured and meticulous – you taught me what it means to minister through service
- Peter Dibble, creative and insightful – your art is a visual song

They not only know their stuff, but they love Jesus and love to serve Him in all they do. This book is a fruit of their ministry.

Thanks to Heath Trampe and Jacob Youmans for inviting me to dance with Tri-Pillar. Your talented writing sets a high mark for those, like me, who follow.

My wife, Liisa, whom I am blessed to have as my partner in the dance of life: you shared all of these experiences with me. Thank you for your unfailing support and encouragement, and for filling the holes in my memory of people, places, and events. Thank you also for creating the wonderful maps in this book.

Thanks to Dale Meyer for writing the Foreword. In the midst of a demanding ministry, you take time for people. Your life is a reflection of the character of Jesus.

Our missionary colleagues in Venezuela became a family to us, and though time and distance have separated us, the bond we share still remains. Thank you for your ministry, your love for the Venezuelan people, and your love for our Lord Jesus. I am still learning from you.

A special thanks to the pastors, leaders, and members of the Lutheran Church of Venezuela. You opened your hearts to us and received us not as strangers, but as brothers and sisters. You taught us to love. May this book, in some small way, serve as a thank-you for all that you gave us.

Foreword

"I didn't read the book but I saw the movie." You've probably said that; I have. I did read *Meeting Ananias* but I actually saw the "movie" first. I met James Tino years ago, in the early 1990s, when I was privileged to visit Venezuela and meet missionaries, tour churches, and get acquainted with the offices of *Cristo para Todas las Naciones* (Christ for All Nations), the Venezuelan title for the work of Lutheran Hour Ministries. Missionary Tino and others took me to places that aren't part of carefully-scripted, pay-thousands-of-dollars tours. We went into a barrio in Caracas. We went into homes for Bible studies. We ate at restaurants that tested my non-spicy, American conditioned diet. I remember one lunch with a local TV personality, a Christian, who told me about homeless children who searched garbage piles for their food. I heard about American military personnel who tended to keep to themselves and not get into Venezuelan communities and culture, a.k.a., squandered mission opportunities. And of course, the missionaries took me to churches – the big, cavernous cathedrals, but more inspiring was the time in the little churches where they faithfully told people about Jesus. That's the "movie" that still plays in my head. Although the names and locations escape me after all these years, I still see the "pictures," the "photographs" recorded in my memory.

Life is pictures. For those blessed with eyesight, our waking hours are one visual after another. Many don't seem memorable: taking the kids to school, walking out of work at the end of the day, cutting grass, and the like – mundane, daily things. Talk to an aged person, though, and those pictured memories are dear and can bring tears to the eyes. These days as never before, what's visual comes not only from our moving through life but also from media. When I was a kid, the very last page in the *Chicago Tribune* was devoted to photos; the rest of the paper was all text. Today, photos are on every newspaper page. Television, computer monitors, smartphones, digital cameras, and all the electronic marvels of our time, flood us with images. In fact, the stream of visuals that come at us is so great that we get numb to the story each photo tells. The torrent makes us spectators, not participants in what we see. I teach preaching at

Concordia Seminary, St. Louis, and regularly ask my class, "What do you think is the most visual of all the media?" The students' answer is dependable: TV or the monitor of their latest gizmo. "Nope," I say. "The most visual of all media is the radio." That draws quizzical looks back and I explain that radio, rightly done, evokes images in the listener's mind that make them a participant in the story. Garrison Keillor is that kind of "visual" radio personality. When you listen to him, you see Lake Wobegon in your mind; you're there, you are part of the story. When I read *Meeting Ananias*, the images from my visit over twenty years ago started popping up in my mind. In fact, the engaging stories recalled pictures for me that I had forgotten. God blessed us with eyes, and they bless our souls.

We pastors and professors do a disservice to people when we reduce the Bible to a series of propositional truths, to one dry, dusty doctrine after another. I don't mean to say that the teachings of the Bible are dry and dusty – anything but! I do mean that sometimes we get so caught up in the intellectual topics of the Bible – the head stuff – that we don't serve the rich story of Jesus down into the heart. Jesus' words are *"Spirit and life"* (John 6:63). *"Sharper than any two-edged sword ... discerning the thoughts and intentions of the heart,"* says Hebrews 4:12 (RSV). God's Word is supposed to go into the ear, to the brain, and down to the heart. How often, and I fear to know, have we failed to go the full 18 inches from head to heart? For that matter, how often have we preached or taught or conversed using theological jargon that doesn't even get into the head because it's so unintelligible to the average layperson? That's a lack of love. There's a favorite church prayer of mine that asks, "...that your Word may not be bound but have free course and be preached to the joy and edifying of Christ's holy people." God is so mysterious and his Son Jesus Christ so abundant in His blessings for us that we not only do a disservice but actually hinder the life-saving Word when we imprison it in theological jargon and head-only truths.

So thank God for these times in which we live! Of course there are reasons – plenty of reasons – to wring our hands and furrow our brows, but God has never made a mistake in placing His people where He wants them to serve. What's great about these times is that the American church is being called back to rediscover the full range of the Gospel. Saving faith is not just words imprisoned on a page or delivered in sermons that sound like college lectures. Christianity never was simply a matter of "information" but true discipleship has always been the "formation" of followers of Jesus Christ. I wonder if the "information only" version of Christianity that has dominated many pulpits and classrooms for a long time is one reason for the decline of mainline churches. Not long ago, I went to one of our seminary librarians and shared something that's been puzzling me. When I was a student, and again 25 years ago during my first teaching stint at Concordia, students came to the first session of a new class with their textbook purchased and in hand. Today, some students come to the first class with no text, others come with a text borrowed from the library, and only a few come having purchased the text. Our librarian explained it to me. She said that some don't buy the book unless they know it will be worth their while; the fact that the professor says it's worth buying doesn't convince them. Then she added a second reason: students learn differently today than they did years ago. Our professors have experienced that, and I could go off and write paragraphs about the change – but that's not the point of these pages. The point is that people today are shaped in all sorts of ways, not just through reading and intellectual thought. To follow Jesus Christ with our whole being, the Word needs to touch all our senses. *"You shall love the LORD your God with all your heart, and with all your soul, and with all your might."* (Deuteronomy 6:5) When we are dealing with words, we want words that will evoke images in our minds. As you read Dr. Tino's work, notice how every Bible passage evokes images and how his narratives do the same. And it's not just visuals. He makes you "hear" sounds, like the wailing of Ramona desperately searching for her lost son Oscar, or the singing of a young boy in the streets. And you can almost feel the penetrating heat as time passes slowly on Ramon's porch, and taste the mangoes eaten after church. Reading Dr. Tino's vivid descriptions even reminded me of a headache I got in Caracas. It is, or at least it was at that time, a city unconcerned about air pollution. After a few days of sucking in exhaust fumes from omnipresent cars, my head started to ache. When Jesus calls disciples to *"Follow me"* (Matthew 4:19), we follow with all that God made us: head, heart, and all our senses.

The great danger in these electronically blessed times is that we will not be discerning about what we take in with our senses. Ask the poor soul struggling to recover from an addiction to pornography about how those pictures worked havoc in his life. What pictures do we followers of Jesus let into our souls? What kind of mental images will be stimulated by our reading? Following Jesus Christ means that we'll monitor the monitors. I recall the Baptist pastor in our town describing how he felt when his mother asked him to take soda bottles back for deposit. In their little country town, the only place to return bottles was the tavern. A pious boy, every time he went into the tavern he was afraid Judgment Day would come and Jesus would find him there! Are the visuals I watch – my passive, spectator viewing – the kind of visuals that I'd want Jesus to sit and watch with me? That's where the reading of the Bible and literature that engages contemporary culture with biblical insights are extremely important and helpful.

The related question is: What visuals do we actively seek with our eyes? Going to church is one part of the answer, but only part. Just as important is going out into the world, going to those who are outside the Lord Jesus Christ, getting to know them and learning their hopes and fears, their joys and their sorrows. *Meeting Ananias* is filled with such stories; that's what missionaries do. I recall another missionary in Venezuela telling me how he would go to places where people gathered, and eavesdrop on their conversations. What he overheard gave him insights as he prepared pamphlets and broadcast scripts to attract people to the Gospel.

But this is not just the job for missionaries. In fact, it shouldn't even be thought of as a "job." God gave us Ten Commandments. The first grouping, the First Table, tells all of us our duties toward God, and the second grouping, the Second Table, describes our duties toward one another. In my experience, church people tend to think that the First Table (commandments one through three or four, depending how you've been taught to number them) are where the Christian life is concentrated. Many Christians take the remaining commandments merely as what to avoid doing during the week. Whoa, back the truck up! The fact is that the commandments that tell us how to relate to others show us how to serve other people in the name of the Servant of Servants, our Lord Jesus Christ. When you involve yourself in appropriate ways with the lives of others, you are serving them and – now comes the great blessing of going into the community – you are compelled to go to God with questions and prayers and repentance. *Dear Lord, what's the Church doing about what I'm seeing in the world? Lord, why isn't the Church doing anything? God, how can you let this suffering happen? God, am I part of the reason this problem exists? Am I too comfortable in my life?* Getting into the lives of people hurting because of the sin in this world drives us to repentance, to forgiveness, and to hope in the One who raised Jesus from the dead. Following me? Serving the desperate problems of humanity – outlined in the Second Table – impels you to God's Word and worship, where the Spirit strengthens faith – the First Table.

Some years ago, I was working my way through a crowded concourse at LaGuardia Airport in New York and heard, "Dr. Meyer!" Soon I was surrounded by half a dozen or so seminarians who had just completed an intensive cross-cultural course in the

Bronx. Like kids holding up their hands in a children's sermon, these future pastors were eager to share with me the faith-stimulating experiences they had with city ministry. Two leaders of the Lutheran Reformation, Philipp Melanchthon and Martin Chemnitz, actually describe Christian service to others as the "true worship" of God (Martin Chemnitz, *Loci Theologici*, Ten Commandments, 716). The visuals of real people in their real lives can change your life.

What are the visuals you are actively taking in? What are the "movies" that are going to be playing in your mind for years to come? One final image from my trip to Venezuela: In one large cathedral, I was fascinated by a glass case containing a statue of Jesus, lying dead after His crucifixion. When I asked for an explanation, my missionary guides told me that's how Jesus is usually depicted in Venezuela: dead, never resurrected. Jesus portrayed to the people as dead but not alive for us. Always the visual of Good Friday, never the visual of Easter. Despair and death, not life and hope. The missionaries were about changing the visuals, about introducing the people to Jesus Christ alive, pouring out abundant hope and leading us to heavenly life. This book is an encouragement for you to get down into it. You'll be a stronger Christian if you look for more than Sunday's stained glass. Better is total discipleship: head, heart, and all our senses, stained glass, *and* the sights of service to others in Jesus' name. Follow Me?

Rev. Dale A. Meyer, Ph.D.
St. Louis, Missouri

The Reason

Where does mission begin? Does it begin on the day of Pentecost? Or does it begin on a mountain in Galilee, where Jesus commissioned the Eleven? Or perhaps much earlier, even as God called out to fallen Man in the Garden, *"Where are you?"* (Genesis 3:9)

For me, the beginning of mission is not found in time, but in a place – the heart of God. Mission begins with the beating of God's heart, because it is who God is. Even as God is Love, and Mercy, and Justice, and Compassion, and Faithfulness, and Truth – just so, God is also Mission. God's desire is for *"all people to be saved and to come to a knowledge of the truth"* (1 Timothy 2:4). Mission is a part of God's being – He cannot do other than to desire the salvation of all, because His nature is to save. Mission begins with the beginning of God.

In His mercy and wisdom, God has called His children to participate in His mission. The mission is never ours – it belongs to God alone, for *"Salvation belongs to our God, who sits on the throne, and to the Lamb."* (Revelation 7:10) The power is not ours.

The result is not ours. What *is* ours is the treasure of the Gospel – the Good News that *"Christ Jesus came into the world to save sinners – of whom I am the worst."* (1 Timothy 1:15) What is ours is the promise of God – *"Never will I leave you; never will I forsake you."* (Hebrews 13:5) What is ours is the mystery of God – the water of Baptism which *"now saves you"* (1 Peter 3:21) and the bread and wine of Holy Communion, *"poured out for many for the forgiveness of sins"* (Matthew 26:28).

What is also ours is the cross of Christ, which stands at the center of God's mission. God's desire to gather all unto Him leads to His own death and resurrection. Through death, God brings life. As God draws us into His mission, He invites us to die. We die to our desires, so that God's desire can be fulfilled. We die to sin, so that we may live to God. We die to ourselves, so that Christ may be manifested through us to others.

In Christ, we who were dead are raised with Him to new life! Raised from death to life through the waters of Baptism (cf. Romans 6:4), we are brought into God's family. We *"once were not a people, but now (we) are the people of God"* (1 Peter 2:10,

NASB) – the Church. God has chosen the Church to be His dwelling place among the nations. Like Israel of old, we have passed through the waters of Baptism and have emerged with the identity of God's own possession. We belong to God.

God's heart beats, and the pulse both draws and sends. As Christ was sent to a world that *"did not receive him"* (John 1:11), the Church sends her own into a world that does not receive them. Yet it may happen that the body of Christ in a place would cease to draw or to send. When that happens, circulation ceases; the lifeblood pools and stagnates, and the body sickens and even dies. But it is not God who has died, it is the church in that place. For the church to be Church, She must pulse with the heartbeat of God – both drawing the nations and sending Her sons and daughters into all the world.

As the Church celebrates the presence of God-among-us in corporate worship, She participates in God's centripetal mission activity of drawing the peoples unto Himself. Quickened and nourished by the life-giving and life-sustaining Word and Sacraments, and empowered by the Spirit, within Her breast beats the heart of God – the *missio Dei*.

Filled and strengthened, we are sent into the world: ***"As the Father has sent Me, I also send you."*** (John 20:21, NASB) The life of the Sent One shapes the attitudes, words, and conduct of those who are sent. In His incarnation, Christ became one of us and walked among us. In the same way, those who are sent will want to become one with the people to whom they are sent. In doing so, they come to know more fully what it means to "die to self," as the missionary learns to step outside of the comfortable boundaries of culture which have defined him or her, and step into the unfamiliar and sometimes uncomfortable lifeways of a new culture.

In His ministry, Jesus brought the full counsel of God to people in ways that were meaningful and comprehensible. Those who are sent will also seek to present the Word of God to the people in meaningful and comprehensible ways.

In His life, Christ did not look to be served, but to serve (cf. Mark 10:45). In the same way, those who are sent do not seek to establish themselves as lord and master, but rather to serve others.

In His death, Christ did not hesitate to sacrifice, giving even His own life for the sake of those to whom He was sent. Those who are sent know that they will be called upon to sacrifice – yes, even to the point of giving up one's own life – for the sake of those to whom they are sent.

After His resurrection, Christ gathered the believers and empowered them by the indwelling of the Holy Spirit. In the same way, the participants in God's mission are empowered by the Holy Spirit, who "calls, gathers, enlightens, and sanctifies the whole Christian church on earth."[1] The goal of mission is not merely individual conversion, but includes their incorporation into the ecclesiastical community. God's mission is carried out through the Church, and leads back to the Church.

Where does mission begin? It begins in the heart of God. Its center is Jesus Christ – His death and resurrection. Its end is triumphal gathering of the saints around the throne, *"from every nation, from all tribes and peoples and languages, ... crying out with a loud voice, 'Salvation belongs to our God who sits on the throne, and to the Lamb!'"* (Revelation 7:9-10, ESV)

---

[1] Luther's Small Catechism, from the explanation to the Third Article of the Apostle's Creed

Introduction

"You used to be a missionary in Venezuela? Wow! What was it like?"

It's a question that my wife and I have heard often enough, yet defies an easy answer. How do you summarize nearly 13 years of ministry?

I was 25 years old when I graduated from the seminary and received my first Call through the placement committee of the Lutheran Church – Missouri Synod as an evangelistic missionary to Venezuela. My wife, Liisa, and I had been married for four years, and she was five months pregnant with our first child. After completing pre-field training, obtaining passports and other documents, and packing our belongings for the international move, the due date was only one month away. It was decided that we would stay in the States until the baby was born and was old enough to travel. Our first daughter, Sonrisa, was born in October 1988. We left for language school in Guatemala in early January 1989. After a brief 12 weeks of language learning, we felt ready to move to Venezuela to begin our ministry, joining a long list of men and women who contributed to the growth of the Lutheran Church of Venezuela.

The Beginnings

The Lutheran Church – Missouri Synod sent the first missionary, Rev. Theophilus Strieter, to begin working in Caracas in 1951. A congregation was soon organized and a school was formed under the direction of missionary Rev. Robert Huebner, who joined Rev. Strieter in 1952. The Zeuch family, Lutheran immigrants from Germany who were making a living as farmers in Monagas State, were also evangelizing in the eastern part of the country. They joined forces with the fledgling Lutheran church in Caracas, and in 1954 Heinrich Zeuch became a Lutheran pastor. In 1956, the Lutheran Church of Venezuela was formally organized.

We arrived in April 1989, just a few weeks after an attempted coup had caused massive rioting in Caracas. After orientation to the country and visits to some of the established congregations, we settled into our new home on the church property in Maturín, which is about 300 miles east of Caracas. Maturín is the capital of Monagas State (Venezuela has 23 states), and is by far the largest city in that part of the country. The church building, recently constructed, had ground floor classrooms and offices, and three apartments on the second floor. The smaller apartment in front was used for church activities. The two larger apartments shared a stairway entrance, and were mirror images of each other. One was occupied by another missionary family who had been in Maturín for ten years. We moved into the other one.

The Maturín congregation was formed in response to the ongoing migration of members from rural congregations into the city. Christian mission work often flourishes in the less populated areas of Venezuela. However, the opportunities for employment and education in such places are minimal, and as a result, the most promising and enterprising individuals usually end up moving to the cities. Unfortunately, those same people are the ones who show the greatest leadership potential in the church, leaving the rural churches with a chronic shortage of qualified and capable leaders.

Team Ministry

Throughout the 1960s and 1970s, Lutheran mission work in Monagas State was focused on the rural areas and small towns. Congregations were quickly established, but suffered from the dearth of leadership and the loss of members to the cities. In Caracas, the other Lutheran mission center, progress was slow due to the challenging urban environment. It was clear that the urbanization of Venezuela would continue for the foreseeable future, and that the rural congregations would continue their slow decline. Missionaries and church leaders in Venezuela wrestled with the problem, and by 1980, they had developed a clear strategy for Lutheran mission work. A team approach was implemented, in which two or more missionaries would work together to build vibrant congregations in the major cities of the country. A few missionaries would continue to minister to the rural congregations without the expectation that those churches would become self-sufficient.

By the time we arrived, the "team strategy" was well established. In Maturín, we joined a team of three missionaries and several Venezuelan deacons (laymen who were trained to lead worship services), and together we ministered to seven small rural congregations scattered around Monagas State, in addition to the larger urban congregation in the city. Throughout the country, other missionary teams were formed in cities like San Félix de Guayana, Puerto Ordaz, Valencia, Caracas, and later Maracay and Barquisimeto. All together, there were 19 Lutheran missionary families in Venezuela.

After four years in Maturín, we were asked to join a new church-planting team in the city of Barquisimeto. We moved there in 1993, and stayed until 2001, when we left Venezuela. Our years in Maturín and Monagas State, though few, were instrumental in shaping us according to God's plan for the rest of our ministry in Venezuela and beyond. We were blessed to work with wise and experienced missionary colleagues, who taught us how to live in Venezuela and how to love her people. We also were privileged to experience the "cradle" of the Lutheran Church of Venezuela, and to meet many of the founding members who were evangelized years ago by the first missionaries.

More than that, though, rural ministry provided us the opportunity to experience unvarnished Venezuelan culture, without the Western trappings that adorn life in the big cities. We got to experience life as it used to be throughout the country, before the landscape was forever changed by the discovery of Venezuelan oil and the onset of massive urbanization. I am convinced that the character of a country is most clearly seen in her rural roots. The experiences of one's forebears is indelibly stamped into the generations that follow, shaping and influencing a people's way of thinking, feeling, and acting long after their rural past is buried and forgotten. Our time in Monagas State allowed us to better understand the heart of all Venezuelans.

Venezuela is a challenging environment for evangelical Christian mission work. In the big cities, work and family pressures, consumerism, materialism, and other dynamics of the urban lifestyle conspire to keep people busy and preoccupied, with little time to contemplate their spiritual condition. Over 90% of the population is nominally Roman Catholic, but the vast majority of her people practice a hybrid version of Catholicism, mixing spiritism and paganism with Catholic customs and beliefs. This makes it difficult to explain Biblical Christianity – words like "sin," "grace," "faith," and even "Jesus" have been co-opted by the popular religious culture, and have taken on meanings that are inimical to Christianity.

Our Ministry in Venezuela

One of God's gifts to our ministry was our children. Venezuelans love children beyond anything we had ever experienced. When we arrived, our baby daughter was a people magnet, and a source of innumerable conversations. Our daughters Gabriela (born in 1990) and Veronica (born in 1992) multiplied the effect. Raising children, caring for children, and talking about children provided us not only with joy, but also with a way to connect with Venezuelan families. Our son Benjamin was born in 1994, during our first year in Barquisimeto, and bonded us in the same way with the people in that city.

Because our children were fair-skinned and light-haired, they drew special attention wherever they went. In church, the youth would take our children and carry them around and care for them throughout the service, allowing Liisa and I to do our part in leading worship. In the rural areas, the children were sure to draw a crowd for church activities. As they grew older, they continued to be a part of the ministry,

attending Sunday School and helping with church activities and work projects. Our ministry in Venezuela
was a family ministry, in every sense of the word.

As a missionary pastor, my duties were centered
on two tasks: evangelism and leadership training. The
goal of a church-planting missionary is to establish a
congregation that is able to sustain and multiply its
own ministry under indigenous leaders. To do this,
there needs to be enough members to support the
ministry, and enough leaders trained to lead the
ministry. In the early stages of a church plant, the
missionary focuses more on evangelism. As the
church grows, the missionary shifts more and more to
training people so that they can assume responsibility
for leading the ministry. An effective church planter
works himself out of a job.

One of the things my wife and I love about the
Venezuelan culture is that people and personal
relationships are a high priority for everyone, all the
time – or so it seems to us. Any time is a good time
for a social gathering. It is not uncommon for a person
on an errand to end up visiting with someone for so
long that they never make it to their destination – even
when the destination is something "important," like a

job interview or a doctor appointment. On the way, they might meet a friend (or make a new friend). Greetings are exchanged, conversation ensues, and before long, people are telling stories – the latest news from the family, or recollections of past experiences, or something to make you laugh. The original objective is set aside because you can go to the doctor or find a job anytime, but the opportunity to be with *these* people in *this* place and at *this* time is unique and special. For the Venezuelan, the important thing is people.

I would like to think a little of that rubbed off on me and my family during the years we spent in Venezuela. Coming from the United States, it was challenging for us to reorient our lives by putting our relationships with others as the number one priority. At the same time, it was refreshing and invigorating on a number of levels, not the least of which was our faith. Now, we see more clearly what it means to be a "community" and the Body of Christ. We feel that we have gained greater insight into God's way of viewing our world, and it starts with this truth: God loves people! He gave everything, even His own life, to restore our relationship with Him so that we can be with Him for eternity.

Not only does God love people, but He also loves working *through* people. He could carry out His will for us through constellations and planets, through apparitions and angels, or even through rocks and trees, and perhaps sometimes He does – it certainly would be easier for Him. But most of the time, God works through people. All of the great heroes of the faith, from Abraham to Moses to David to Peter and Paul, were people that God did not "need" to accomplish His purposes, but whom He chose to use nevertheless. God led the nation of Israel through human leaders. He gave us His Word through people like the prophets and apostles. He has entrusted the message of salvation to us, His followers. Why does God insist on working in us and through us, when we so often make a mess of things? The reason is that our shared life in Christ is the canvas on which, with masterful artistry, God paints His self-portrait. Each of our lives, and the life of every Christian, is a brush stroke on that canvas.

We were privileged to see some of God's brush strokes in Venezuela, and the result was both unexpected and amazing. Like a 3-D movie, it can be viewed without the special glasses, but when you put them on, everything takes on new vibrancy and depth. Seeing God at work in the lives of people from a different culture was like putting on 3-D glasses. Before we went to Venezuela, we understood God through the Scriptures, but only from our own cultural perspective. As we participated in the faith and life of the Venezuelan Lutherans, we saw a new dimension of God's self-portrait.

God reveals Himself in the lives of His people. Their stories are *His* stories. It is my prayer that as you read about God at work in the lives of His people in Venezuela, you too will see another dimension of God's self-portrait.

Rev. James Tino, Ph.D.
Epiphany 2014

Maps

Venezuela

Monagas State

Genesis 12:1-3

The LORD had said to Abram, "Go from your country, your people and your father's household to the land I will show you.

>"I will make you into a great nation,
>>and I will bless you;
>I will make your name great,
>>and you will be a blessing.
>I will bless those who bless you,
>>and whoever curses you I will curse;
>and all peoples on earth
>>will be blessed through you."

A Life of Faith

Seeing what happens when we follow God's call

I leaned my head back into the chair, squeezing my eyes shut to hold back the tears. As the plane lifted off, I could no longer stop them from flowing. I looked at my wife over the heads of our children; she was crying too. Though we were both filled with heartache at leaving our home in Venezuela, sharing the pain gave each of us a small measure of comfort.

That was the second time I cried on an airplane. The first was 13 years earlier, when we left our home in the United States to move to Venezuela. At that time, I never would have imagined that returning to the States would mean leaving home, again.

Back when I started college, I wasn't even sure that I wanted to be a pastor. I felt called[2] to full-time ministry, but was not immediately drawn to the

---

[2] In this book, the word "Call," when capitalized, refers to the divine call received by ordained clergy. When it is not capitalized, "call" refers to the Christian vocation.

pastoral office. I experimented with youth ministry, deaf ministry, and every other kind of ministry that I could find time for during my college years. However, none of those really appealed to me, and by the time graduation rolled around, it seemed that God was pointing me to the seminary and the pastoral ministry.

Seminary graduates in the Lutheran church are placed into their first Calls by committee. One of the tools that the committee uses to match graduates with Calls is a self-evaluation, which asks the person to grade areas of interest on a scale of 1 to 5. Figuring that the Holy Spirit knows me better than I know myself, I ranked everything on the list as a 3.

Next thing I knew, I was being interviewed for an overseas missionary assignment! I told the interviewers that I was not particularly interested in Hispanic work, that I would prefer ministry in a rural or small-town setting – and that I did not care to be hot.

On "Call Night," when all the graduates receive their first Calls. I lined up with the rest of my classmates. With an eager assembly of parents, relatives, and friends watching, one by one we came forward to discover where we would begin our ministry as pastors. Iowa. Nebraska. Michigan. Illinois. "Hawaii" drew some oohs and aahs. Finally, my turn came ("T" was near the end of the alphabet, even then.) *"James Tino – evangelistic missionary to Venezuela."*

Wait – *where?* Venezuela? Unbelievable! I didn't know Spanish, didn't want to be hot, and couldn't even find Venezuela on a map. *This was where God was calling me?*

I could have turned down the Call; seminary graduates have that option. I could have requested reassignment to a ministry in the United States. I could have protested that the Call was a complete mismatch; that I wanted to stay near my family; that I had no skills which would indicate I was suited for a ministry in Venezuela. But I didn't. I still believed that God knows me better than I know myself, and that this was His call on my life.

And it was. The 13 years that we spent in Venezuela were the richest, most rewarding years of ministry in my life thus far. They were not necessarily easy years, but my wife and I grew to love Venezuela and her people with a heartfelt, enduring love. The ministry there was sometimes frustrating, sometimes exhilarating, and always challenging. I was introduced to a world that I never before imagined – a world where people think differently, act differently, talk differently, and live differently than what I was accustomed to. It was, quite simply, amazing! Becoming a cross-cultural missionary introduced me to a world I would have otherwise never known.

When God called Abram, He said, *"Go from your country, your people and your father's household to the land I will show you."* (Genesis 12:1) God was calling Abram to be a cross-cultural missionary! We often read right over that verse, in a hurry to get to the promise that follows: *"I will make you into a great nation ... all peoples on earth will be blessed through you."* (verses 2-3) We know the end of the story – how God miraculously built the nation of Israel from the unexpected offspring of Abram and Sarai – so the promise is meaningful for us. But I bet Abram got stuck on that very first verse. After all, when he heard these instructions from God he didn't know how the story would end. I'm convinced those words really didn't register with him, at least not at first. When God said, *"Go from your country, your people and your father's household,"* Abram was probably thinking, *Wait – did I hear You right? You're calling me to just pick up and leave my family, my people, and everything that's familiar and comfortable – to go off to some unknown land?!* I can certainly identify with the kinds of doubts and fears that must have been in his heart. He probably had a list of reasons he could have given to God for why he should remain right where he was. But he didn't. God called, and Abram went. He stepped out in faith.

As you follow the Lord, at some point He is going to ask you to step out in faith. He is going to place in you the desire to do something you never before considered doing – whether it's a career change, a new ministry, more education, relocation, or something else. As you contemplate it, you will realize that if you do this thing, your whole life will change. The temptation to resist that call of faith will be strong, because change can be scary and uncertain. There are good reasons for maintaining the status quo. But know this: If you do not step out in faith, you will most likely regret it.

As I speak to congregations and other groups of people about mission work, I am surprised by the number of people who tell me, "You know, God called me to do this or that many years ago, but for one reason or another, I never did it. I have always regretted it." Sometimes I ask them what the reasons were for not following that particular call of God in their lives. Most of the time, their reasons sound to me more like excuses. "I didn't want to leave my job." "I didn't want to uproot the family." "It didn't seem to be a good time." "I thought I would do it later in life." These all boil down to two main deterrents: Fear and Inconvenience.

The people of Israel were plagued by the same issues. After they left the familiarity of Egypt, they quickly forgot their former status as slaves and complained because their food was not coming to them in the usual way (Numbers 11:1-15). Gathering manna was inconvenient. And when they finally were poised to enter the Promised Land, the Israelites again longed for Egypt because they were afraid, certain that they would be slaughtered when they entered Canaan (Numbers 14:1-12). As we look at Israel's example, it becomes clear that "fear" is a lack of trust in God, and "inconvenience" is selfishness. There – I said it. People are living with God's second-best for their lives because they do not trust God, or because they are self-centered, or both. Lots of people. And I've seen how much they regret it.

Are you living with regret? There are a lot of things in my life that I feel bad about: words spoken in haste, missed opportunities, times when I did the very thing that I was determined not to do. Sometimes the feeling is so strong it keeps me awake at night. But one thing I do not regret is accepting the Call to Venezuela. For perhaps the first time in my life, I truly stepped out in faith, trusting that the Lord really *did* know me better than I knew myself. I put aside my doubts and my fears and jumped – trusting in God. It was a decision that changed my life in ways that I couldn't have imagined or predicted, and I've never regretted it. Never.

People who learn about my mission work often comment to me, "I could never do what you do." I accept that, as long as they also accept that I could never do what *they* do! God has uniquely equipped each of us for the things He wants us to do, for the ***"good works, which God prepared in advance for us to do"*** (Ephesians 2:10). The things God has prepared for me to do are no bigger or smaller, and no more or less important, than what He has prepared for you to do. *All* of God's works are perfect and beautiful and admirable. Each of us has a crucial role to play. But in order to follow His call on your life, you need to live a life of faith.

Living a life of faith is different from *faithful living*. Faithful living means that you are diligent in discipleship – practicing the spiritual disciplines, growing in faith, and serving the Lord and others with your time, talents, and treasures. All Christians should practice faithful living.

But a life of faith is something else entirely. It begins with security. Part of our human condition is that we crave security, because security gives us the illusion of control. When we feel secure, then we are confident in our ability to "handle things," whatever that might mean. Predictability gives us a sense of security. Money often gives a sense of security. Routine gives us a sense of security.

A life of faith is unpredictable. It feels insecure. It begins with an openness to the Lord's leading in your life, whenever and however that may come, and it ends in places that we would never expect. A life of faith means that you will need to be satisfied with a different kind of security – the security of knowing that the Lord is with you, and that is, quite simply, enough. *He* is what you lean upon, instead of the security of your job or family or bank account or retirement fund. This might mean that you spend long stretches of time "living in the mystery," as a missionary colleague of mine likes to say, referring to the mystery of not knowing where this is all leading, what is coming next, or even if you are doing the right thing. A life of faith has no promises to grasp hold of, except this one: *"I am with you always, to the very end of the age"* (Matthew 28:20). At the end of the day, a life of faith is demonstrated by your willingness to say "yes" to God, above all else.

What will happen when you jump into a life of faith? Even if things do not work out smoothly or in a way you would have hoped, at least you will know that you took that crucial step of faith. You will have the experience of living with no (man-made) safety net. Your faith will be stretched. Your prayer life will be greatly deepened, because when all you have is the Lord, you spend a lot of time in conversation with Him! And who knows? That step of faith may open to you a world that you otherwise would have never known!

What has God called you to do? What is the passion that is burning in your heart, the idea that gets your blood pumping and your mind racing and your feet tapping? Will you take the leap of faith and jump into an as-yet-unknown world of learning and discovery and joy – and yes, even hardship? Or will you let Fear and Inconvenience claim another victim? Remember that you are uniquely gifted by God for a reason – to do the things that He has prepared for *you* to do. It's not too late – it's *never* too late – to start living a life of faith. Ask Abraham.

No regrets. I can live with that.

Acts 9:10-19

In Damascus there was a disciple named Ananias. The Lord called to him in a vision, "Ananias!"

"Yes, Lord," he answered.

The Lord told him, "Go to the house of Judas on Straight Street and ask for a man from Tarsus named Saul, for he is praying. In a vision he has seen a man named Ananias come and place his hands on him to restore his sight."

"Lord," Ananias answered, "I have heard many reports about this man and all the harm he has done to your holy people in Jerusalem. And he has come here with authority from the chief priests to arrest all who call on your name."

But the Lord said to Ananias, "Go! This man is my chosen instrument to proclaim my name to the Gentiles and their kings and to the people of Israel. I will show him how much he must suffer for my name."

Then Ananias went to the house and entered it. Placing his hands on Saul, he said, "Brother Saul, the Lord – Jesus, who appeared to you on the road as you were coming here – has sent me so that you may see again and be filled with the Holy Spirit." Immediately, something like scales fell from Saul's eyes, and he could see again. He got up and was baptized, and after taking some food, he regained his strength.

Meeting Ananias

Seeing the needs of others

Caracas, Venezuela has one of the best subway systems in the world. "The Metro" (as it is called) is clean, modern, efficient, and inexpensive – everything that a developing nation is not. When I lived in Venezuela, whenever I was in Caracas, I rode the metro. I usually took the connector bus to the *Sabana Grande* entrance, where there was a blind woman who sat on a small stool, selling candy and cigarettes from a tray on her lap. You could hardly miss her, really. When she sensed that people were nearby, her nasal "hawker's cry" could be heard for blocks.

I often wondered how that blind woman managed to make change for her customers. At that time, coins were not in circulation in Venezuela. All of the money was paper money – same size, same shape – and the only difference I could see between the bills was the color, and the number printed on the front. How does a blind woman make change? I had to know. One day, on my way to the metro, I bought a sucker from the woman. She told me that it cost five *bolívares*, so I gave her a 20, just to see what she would do. She carefully ran her fingers over the bill, and gave me 15 *bolívares* in change!

I was amazed, but in a way, the whole situation also kind of made me sad. In the United States, blindness is definitely a physical challenge, but many blind people are able to go to school, get a job, and lead relatively normal lives. In Venezuela, blindness is a debilitating handicap. Even gifted and enterprising people, like the woman at the metro station, are relegated to begging for food at the margins of society.

Physical blindness is bad, but spiritual blindness is worse. The physically blind know that they are blind, but the spiritually blind do not. The physically blind know that they cannot do everything on their own. They are aware that they need help from time to time. The spiritually blind, on the other hand, do not even know that they need help, particularly from the One who came to rescue them from their blindness. They are unaware of their sin and of their desperate need for a Savior.

The apostle Paul experienced both kinds of blindness. Before his conversion, when he was known as Saul, he was spiritually blind. In his blindness, Saul was opposed to all who followed Jesus. In fact, it was his life's mission to get rid of the Jesus-followers. But then... he met Jesus! At a moment when he least expected it – walking along the road to Damascus – he met Jesus. Saul's spiritual blindness was removed in an instant, and in its place, God made him physically blind by putting something like scales over his eyes. Saul remained blind for three days, fasting and praying. Did he ask God to remove his blindness? I know I would have. Although God could have relieved Saul of his blindness directly, He chose to send an unlikely healer – Ananias. Ananias had his own "blind spot" – he did not see any possible way that Saul could be used by God. The blind healing the blind!

It seems to me that we are in the midst of a blindness epidemic. The spiritually blind are all around us, increasing in number day by day. At the same time, scales seem to be descending over the eyes of Christians, blinding us to the urgent need to share Jesus with others. Do we see the blind? Who will go to them? Who will pray for them? Who will be their Ananias? Or do we need God to send Ananias to us?

I met Ananias. It was during my time in language school in Antigua, Guatemala. Since I spoke very little Spanish, the profusion of beggars and hustlers crowding the narrow cobblestone streets was over-whelming to me. I felt threatened, alone, and insecure; moving quickly through the streets, I tried to avoid the panhandlers. So many needs! I could not possibly give money to everyone, so I gave money to no one.

One day, while walking down a relatively quiet street in Antigua, I heard the voice of a young boy singing. It sounded like the soloist of a boy's choir – pure, sweet soprano tones, echoing off the stucco walls lining the streets. It was beautiful, and drew me like a siren's song. I could not see where the sound was coming from, but as I walked, I suddenly came upon the boy. He was blind, perhaps 12 years old, standing in the recessed doorway of one of the buildings, and holding in his hand the proverbial tin cup. As I passed, he rattled the cup gently. I did not put anything in it.

I continued on my way, the bell-like tones fading away until they finally stopped. At that moment the scales started to fall from my eyes. *What was I thinking?*, I berated myself. *Why am I so selfish with my money?* That boy was no charlatan, no hustler, no con artist. He was just a poor, blind boy, in need of money to buy food and clothes, in need of the love of Jesus.

I turned around and hurried back to the place where I remembered seeing the boy, but I could not find him. The song had ended. I watched and listened for him for the next several weeks, but did not see him again. I never talked to the boy, never learned his name. But for me, his name is Ananias.

What will it take for us to see – really see – with Jesus' eyes? As He looks on our world, God isn't seeing the things that we focus on. He's not watching our bank accounts or our fashion selections. He's not keeping track of the things people have done to take advantage of us, hurt our feelings, or do us wrong. He sees the hurting, the lonely, the lost, the blind. He sees people who need help. He sees people waiting for Ananias.

Luke 10:30-37

Jesus said: "A man was going down from Jerusalem to Jericho, when he was attacked by robbers. They stripped him of his clothes, beat him and went away, leaving him half dead. A priest happened to be going down the same road, and when he saw the man, he passed by on the other side. So too, a Levite, when he came to the place and saw him, passed by on the other side. But a Samaritan, as he traveled, came where the man was; and when he saw him, he took pity on him. He went to him and bandaged his wounds, pouring on oil and wine. Then he put the man on his own donkey, brought him to an inn and took care of him. The next day he took out two denarii and gave them to the innkeeper. 'Look after him,' he said, 'and when I return, I will reimburse you for any extra expense you may have.'

"Which of these three do you think was a neighbor to the man who fell into the hands of robbers?"

The expert in the law replied, "The one who had mercy on him."

Jesus told him, "Go and do likewise."

i Exam

Seeing faith in action

Pablo needed glasses. There weren't many men in our small congregation in Rio Chiquito, so I tried to encourage the ones who came to church by giving them an active role in the worship service – usually reading one of the Scripture lessons. Pablo could read, which was a big plus. But his eyesight wasn't very good, so it was hard for him to read the text with any kind of accuracy or fluency. He often declined the invitation to be a reader due to his eyesight, and the job was passed on to one of the many women in the congregation. This was embarrassing for him. Additionally, I had noticed that Pablo was struggling to read the newspaper, which was one of his favorite pastimes, and which also gave him a certain status in the village – not everyone could read, and the one who read the paper became a go-to person for news and information. If he didn't get glasses, I felt certain that his self-esteem would be affected. His confidence as a reader in church was already starting to erode, and I could even foresee a time when Pablo would stop coming to church altogether.

Distorted vision causes all kinds of problems. Whether or not we wear corrective lenses, all of us have a worldview "lens" which determines how we "see" things – how we understand reality. The way we are raised, our life experiences, level of education, culture, and even the language we speak all have a part in shaping our worldview. For example, if a person is raised in a loving family, he or she will probably tend to be open and trusting with others. However, if a person is raised in an abusive situation, that experience will have a deep and lasting impact on the way he or she interacts with other people. The greatest challenge in all of this is that no one is really aware of their own lens! We tend to assume that the way we understand reality is the same way that everyone else sees things – which, of course, is not true.

Getting new glasses seemed like a simple and straightforward process to me, but from Pablo's perspective, it was not so easy. There were a number of obstacles that needed to be overcome. The little mountain community of Rio Chiquito was over an hour away from Maturín, the nearest large city, and by public transportation the journey took over two and a half hours each way. Going to Maturín for glasses would be an all-day affair, and at least one day of missed work for Pablo. Then, there was the cost of the glasses themselves to consider. There was also the added complication that Pablo did not know his way around the city, and he was afraid of getting lost or becoming a victim of swindlers. And finally, Pablo had no idea how to go about obtaining glasses. I'm not sure that he had ever been to see any doctor, much less an optometrist.

Have you ever been in a situation where you felt like you were so out of your element that you just wished someone could be there to walk alongside you and guide you? The more I thought about all the obstacles that Pablo faced in this situation, the more I realized that this was not something he would be able to do on his own. Verbal directions, encouragement, and even money wouldn't be enough for him. He needed someone who knew the system – someone to come alongside him and help him through it. If I wanted Pablo to succeed, I knew that I would need to take a more active role in helping him get his glasses.

Little by little, we devised a plan that would address most of the difficulties. Pablo would travel with me back to Maturín one Sunday after worship. He would stay at our house overnight. In the morning, he and I would go together to the optometrist, and I would pay for the glasses. Then Pablo would take the bus back home to Rio Chiquito in the afternoon.

Are we able to identify the people around us who are in need, or do we assume that if people need help, they will ask for it? God wants us to see the world as He sees it – from His perspective. What do we see as we look through *our* worldview lenses? When God looks at our world, He sees people who are hurting, lonely, lost, and confused. When we see them, are we willing to help out? Or do we make excuses as to why we can't be bothered? If a person needs help, there are really only two ways to respond – and both are reflected in the parable of the Good Samaritan. The first way is to "pass by on the other side" (cf. Luke 10:31, 32) – pretend you didn't notice, and keep going on with your life. The second way is to go attend to the one in need (verses 33-35) – to stop what you are doing, and help.

On the designated Sunday afternoon, Pablo returned with me to Maturín. As we prepared for the
next day, I tried to anticipate the kinds of things that
might go wrong. For some reason it occurred to me
that Pablo might be tripped up when asked to try on
frames, and mistake the frames for the finished
glasses. So several times, I rehearsed the procedure
that he would follow at the optometrist. I made a point
of emphasizing that at first, he would try on some
frames without any lenses. I warned him that he
would not see a difference in his vision until the
doctor put the lenses in the frames. I imagined how
embarrassing it might be for him if he did not
understand that frames are not glasses. If he felt
humiliated, then the whole plan could fall apart. But if
we could get his vision corrected, I had hopes that
Pablo would regain his confidence and maintain his
self-esteem. He would be able to continue as a source
of news and information in the village, and he could
read the Scripture lessons during worship. He would
be able to see the world – and the Word – with greater
clarity. And I believed that he could even become a
leader in the congregation.

The Big Day arrived, and together we went to the optometrist. The doctor performed the eye exam, which went well. Pablo was feeling confident. So far, so good! Then the doctor said, "Sit down over there, and choose the frames that you like. You can look at yourself in the mirror."

Pablo sat next to the frames, bringing a newspaper with him. He tried on a pair of frames, then looked at the newspaper. *Uh-oh,* I thought, *he's doing it.* He tried on another pair, and looked at the newspaper again. I tried to intervene: "Remember that the doctor is still working on your lenses." Pablo looked at me, and then continued his routine – frames, newspaper, then on to the next pair of frames. Finally he announced quite loudly, "None of these glasses are doing anything for my vision!" Others in the office started to chuckle. Cringing, I explained once again that the frames merely hold the lenses, and the lenses aren't in them yet. I encouraged him to just pick the frames that he liked best, and we would give them to the doctor to make them work properly. Finally, Pablo chose some frames, and the appointment was over. The glasses would be ready in the afternoon. Mission accomplished!

Pablo got *his* glasses, but how do we get *God's* glasses? We acquired our natural worldview from our parents when we were children, and we learn to see things from God's perspective in much the same way. A child learns his parents' worldview by being around them, watching, listening, and imitating. When we read the Bible, when we participate in regular worship, when we meet with others to study the Word of God, we are entering God's world – hanging around God, so to speak. As we read, study, and worship, we contemplate His thoughts. We observe His actions. The more we do these things, the more we become like Him. His Word and Spirit shape in us the mind of Christ. His words become our words; His thoughts become our thoughts; and His actions become our actions. We find the Good Samaritan growing within us.

Some Christians never really get God's lenses because they never "go all in" for Jesus. They tend to avoid Bible study classes because they don't want to seem ignorant, or possibly be embarrassed, by asking questions about the Bible. They don't want to go to church too often, because it might be uncomfortable to try to explain their faith to their friends. They rarely stop to help the one in need, and so they miss out on discovering the joy of service.

What difference would it make if we – all of us – were wearing God's lenses? What if every Christian were the Good Samaritan? At some time or another, everyone needs a helping hand. The new Christian needs someone to walk beside them and guide them in the faith. They need someone to worship with them, because for a new believer, church can be intimidating. The experienced Christian needs encouragement, too. Sometimes making God-pleasing decisions is tough, and we can all benefit from support and direction. Life is full of problems and pitfalls, and no one is able to do it alone. And those who are not Christians need someone to stop, bind up their wounds, and bring them to our Father's house where they can be healed by the Great Physician.

For too many of us, Christianity is just a tradition, a Sunday habit, or a routine, rather than a lifestyle. Yet the Scripture is clear:

> **What good is it, my brothers and sisters, if someone claims to have faith but has no deeds? Can such faith save them? Suppose a brother or a sister is without clothes and**

daily food. If one of you says to them, "Go in peace; keep warm and well fed," but does nothing about their physical needs, what good is it? In the same way, faith by itself, if it is not accompanied by action, is dead. (James 2:14-17)

Christianity without action is like a pair of frames without the lenses. We may look different, but it doesn't change the way we see things. We have the appearance of being changed, but our vision has not been adjusted. When we are immersed in the things of God, His worldview lenses are fit into the framework of our Christianity. But if we are not doers of the Word, then all we have are empty frames.

Pablo got his glasses, and they made all the difference in the world for him. He became a devout reader *and* doer of the Word, and that's how he got his *real* glasses – the ones with God's lenses in the frames.

2 Corinthians 4:1-12

Therefore, since through God's mercy we have this ministry, we do not lose heart. Rather, we have renounced secret and shameful ways; we do not use deception, nor do we distort the word of God. On the contrary, by setting forth the truth plainly we commend ourselves to everyone's conscience in the sight of God. And even if our gospel is veiled, it is veiled to those who are perishing. The god of this age has blinded the minds of unbelievers, so that they cannot see the light of the gospel that displays the glory of Christ, who is the image of God. For what we preach is not ourselves, but Jesus Christ as Lord, and ourselves as your servants for Jesus' sake. For God, who said, "Let light shine out of darkness," made his light shine in our hearts to give us the light of the knowledge of God's glory displayed in the face of Christ.

But we have this treasure in jars of clay to show that this all-surpassing power is from God and not from us. We are hard pressed on every side, but not crushed; perplexed, but not in despair; persecuted, but not abandoned; struck down, but not destroyed. We always carry around in our body the death of Jesus, so that the life of Jesus may also be revealed in our body. For we who are alive are always being given over to death for Jesus' sake, so that his life may also be revealed in our mortal body. So then, death is at work in us, but life is at work in you.

Hidden Treasure

Seeing a reason for suffering

Pastor, why does God allow suffering and pain? That's the question I'm often asked when tragedy strikes – not just the tragedies that make the news, but especially the ones that don't. A young woman now confined to a wheelchair for the rest of her life. A pastor who lost his child to suicide. A missionary couple whose children are both severely disabled. A mother who lost her courageous battle with cancer. A family torn apart by alcoholism. These are the real-life situations of people I know – people who love Jesus with all their might – people who are in worship every Sunday. We know and accept that bad things happen; we just don't think it should happen to *them*. Why does God so often allow His people to end up in such miserable conditions? Why is the Christian life often just plain difficult?

We shouldn't be surprised that it's difficult. In 2 Corinthians 4:1, God tells us, ***"do not lose heart."*** Those words remind us that Christian ministry – and

Christian life – will not be easy. After all, if it was going to be easy, then why would we need encouragement not to lose heart? The reality is that if you are a Jesus-follower, then it's going to be a rough ride. And yet, even knowing this, the question remains: Why do God's people suffer? I started to find the answers in La Morrocoya.

There were no clocks in La Morrocoya. On Sunday afternoons, the people would know it was time for church when they saw in the distance the dust cloud that was raised by my vehicle as I drove in. The mothers would gather their children, scrub them up and send them to church, and then the adults would get themselves ready. So it ended up that I always had about an hour between the sending of the dust signal, and the arrival of the first children at church.

In the meantime, I spent my time at Matilda's. Matilda's house was a traditional stick-and-mud home, a remnant of the "old" La Morrocoya. At some time in the past, the town of La Morrocoya had been flooded. The church, which was built of sturdy concrete, was unaffected by the floodwaters. The stick-and-mud houses, though, were severely damaged when the waters came. In due time, the government rebuilt the town, laying out the streets in neat rows and providing cinder block homes with cement foundations. Matilda stayed in her original home, near the church. She was one of the founding members of Good Shepherd Lutheran – old but sturdy, a faithful woman of God, years of hardship etched onto her leathery face.

Matilda was also toothless. I mention this because teeth make an important contribution to one's pronunciation. At that time in my ministry, I was still learning Spanish. For those who are learning a new language and trying to improve their listening and comprehension skills, I highly recommend spending an hour a week talking to a toothless person. I figured that once I could understand Matilda's Spanish, I could understand anyone's Spanish. I was right.

Learning a new language is a humbling experience. Small children laugh at your childish mistakes. Adults assume that your intellectual capacities are on par with your language skills. To learn a language – really learn it – you need to be willing to set aside pride, ego, and self-reliance, and become something less than you otherwise imagine yourself to be.

Matilda did an admirable job of helping me to do just that.

To help make ends meet, Matilda sold *teticas* – homemade juice, poured into plastic baggies and then frozen – sort of like a freeze-pop. As I sat in her tiny home on a handmade wooden chair and visited, children from the neighborhood would come to her door to buy *teticas*.

I watched the transaction on numerous occasions. At that time, as a grand experiment, the government of Venezuela had replaced all metal coins with paper bills – small bills, like Monopoly® money. The children would come to Matilda's door with their miniature bills in hand. Matilda would give them their treat and take the bills. After the children had left, she would put the money in her hiding place, which was a small clay pot that stood with other, similar vessels on the crude wooden shelf above the stove. It was a potbellied little jug with a narrow neck. Matilda would tightly roll the bills and then pop them into the jug.

I could imagine the tiny bills unrolling as soon as they got past the neck of the jug, which made me wonder: *How does she get the money out? Was there a stopper in the bottom of the jug?* I could not see one. *Tweezers?* Maybe, if she was patient. I always saw the bills go in, but never saw them come out. The jug must have been stuffed with miniature money.

One Sunday afternoon, as our conversation lagged, I decided to solve the mystery. "Matilda," I said, "I know where you keep the money from the *teticas*, and I'm not going to tell anyone. I have seen you putting the bills into that potbellied jug. But what I can't figure out is, how do you get them out? When you want to spend it, you know." I didn't want her to think that I was after her money.

Matilda looked at me like I was a simpleton. I was getting used to that. "Pastor," she said, "when I want the money, I just break the jar."

Why couldn't I figure that out? The jar was a simple, common, everyday vessel – a dime-a-dozen sort of thing, made valuable only because of what it contained. Of course she would break the jar to get the money!

The answer was obvious, but I couldn't see it. As Christians, we often wonder why bad things happen to us, why life is so hard, why we suffer pain and hardship and trials of all kinds. We feel that God should bless us by making our lives easier. After all, aren't we God's chosen people? Doesn't He want us to enjoy the blessings of life? Doesn't God want us to be examples of the new life that we experience in Christ?

Perhaps we have overlooked this verse: *"But we have this treasure in jars of clay to show that this all-surpassing power is from God and not from us."* (verse 7) God fills us, stuffing our clay pots full of the treasures of His grace. But there's a reason that He puts the treasure in earthen vessels – a reason that we would rather avoid. The reason is that earthen vessels are easy to break.

The fact is, God wants the world to see Jesus, and we are His chosen instruments. God fills us with the treasure of the Gospel of Christ, but there's only one way to let the treasure out. We *must* be broken. To show Christ, we must be willing to die to ourselves, so that others can see Jesus. When that happens – when we are broken – it is clear that the surpassing power really is from God. It's not from ourselves at all. We are simple clay pots, blessed with treasure inside. To be broken is our highest calling, because through the shards of our broken lives, the treasure shines forth.

We are hard pressed on every side, but not crushed; perplexed, but not in despair; persecuted, but not abandoned; struck down, but not destroyed. ... For we who are alive are always being given over to death for Jesus' sake, so that his life may also be revealed in our mortal body. (verses 8, 9, and 11)

We are given over to death for Jesus' sake. Those words give away one of God's secrets: He loves to work with dead things! He created Man from the dead dust of the ground. He brought forth the nation of Israel from the dead womb of Sarah. Jonah was brought back from the dead – out of the belly of the great fish – to bring new life to Nineveh. Jesus rose triumphant from the grave. Dead things have no power, no ability; there is nothing they can do on their own. God works with dead things because when He does, there is no doubt Who is at work! The power is from God, and not from ourselves.

Paul said, *"For what we preach is not ourselves, but Jesus Christ as Lord, and ourselves as your servants for Jesus' sake."* (verse 5) But the truth of the matter is that we often *do* preach ourselves. We want to be a living testimony of what it's like to follow Jesus, but only through ways that are easy and convenient for us. We want our lives to be models of perfection: pain-free, trouble-free, stress-free, and worry-free. Hardship bothers us, because we don't know how to reconcile the pain in our lives with a God who loves us and who can do anything for us. Life should be perfect when we follow Jesus. Right?

Wrong. If others are to see Jesus, then we must be broken. Pride, ego, and self-sufficiency must go. There is no other way to show that the power is of God, and not of ourselves. There is no stopper in the bottom; the treasure of the Gospel cannot be extracted with tweezers. There's only one way to do it – brokenness.

I used to wonder why God allows suffering. I see it now. Matilda explained it to me – and she did it without any teeth.

John 5:1-9

Some time later, Jesus went up to Jerusalem for one of the Jewish festivals. Now there is in Jerusalem near the Sheep Gate a pool, which in Aramaic is called Bethesda and which is surrounded by five covered colonnades. Here a great number of disabled people used to lie – the blind, the lame, the paralyzed. One who was there had been an invalid for thirty-eight years. When Jesus saw him lying there and learned that he had been in this condition for a long time, he asked him, "Do you want to get well?"

"Sir," the invalid replied, "I have no one to help me into the pool when the water is stirred. While I am trying to get in, someone else goes down ahead of me."

Then Jesus said to him, "Get up! Pick up your mat and walk." At once the man was cured; he picked up his mat and walked.

Ana's Bible

Seeing the Word of God as our treasure

Did you ever have something that you just could not part with? Two of our children kept their "blankies" until well into their teen years. The blankets, once soft and smooth and comforting, were by that time little more than tattered rags. Still, no one wanted to part with them because even in their precarious condition, they held memories – precious memories of childhood, and love, and warmth, and security.

I don't think that's what was going on with the paralyzed man who was healed by Jesus in John chapter 5. He had been an invalid for 38 years. Each day, his family or friends would carry him on his pallet to the Bethesda pool, and each night they would carry him home. He probably ate on the pallet, slept on the pallet, and lived on the pallet. Yet I doubt that the paralyzed man looked at his pallet in the same way that my kids looked at their blankets, as a treasure-trove of precious memories. The pallet contained memories, all right – memories of lying in the dust, crippled, looking up at the "regular" people walking by. Memories of not being able to take care of one's own needs. Memories of helplessness. Memories of feeling useless, unwanted, a burden on those you love.

So it's hard to imagine that the man would want to keep his pallet once he was healed. And yet, that's just what Jesus told him to do. ***"Rise, take up your pallet, and walk."*** (John 5:8) Why should he take up his pallet? Why not just "Rise, and walk?" Certainly Jesus was not concerned that the man might be accused of littering if he left his grimy old pallet at Bethesda. No, that bed of bad memories would best be left behind.

Ana helped me understand why Jesus might have told the man to take his pallet with him. Ana was an old, old woman, brown and wrinkled – a walnut with white hair. She lived alone with her young grand-daughter deep in the Venezuelan countryside. Her home was accessible only by foot. Occasionally on Sundays, Ana would make her way out to the blacktop road, where she would wait. On Sunday mornings, myself or another missionary would drive that road on our way to Rio Chiquito – a tiny congregation deep in the mountains. We had to keep a sharp eye out for

Ana, and if she was there, we would give her a ride to church. After church, we would give her a ride back to her spot on the road.

One Sunday, after services had ended in Rio Chiquito, Ana asked if instead of dropping her off at her usual spot, could we bring her with us all the way back to Maturín. She had to do an errand that could only be done in the big city. We brought her back to our house, and eventually convinced her to join us for dinner and spend the night. Ana was clearly out of her element in the city, in a house with electric lights and running water and several rooms. We did our best to ease her awkwardness and make her comfortable.

During the evening, it seemed clear that Ana had something on her mind, so I sat around and made myself available, in case she wanted to talk. She eventually worked up enough courage to ask: "Pastor, if it would not be too much trouble, and if you will pardon my asking, would it be possible, just by chance, that you might have a Bible for me?"

"Of course!" I responded, both relieved at the simplicity of her request and touched by her humility. "But, don't you already have a Bible?" I asked. She always brought a Bible with her to church.

"I do, but mine is all worn out."

In order to get a Bible of the same version that she was accustomed to using, I asked to see her old one. Sure enough, the hard cover of her Bible was worn almost completely through. It was obviously well-used, and I quickly produced a brand-new replacement.

She received the Bible with evident joy. Embarrassed by her effusive thanks, I nervously opened her old Bible. To my surprise, the pages inside were brilliant white, untouched – they even crackled like it was the first time the book had been opened.

"Ana," I said, "the pages inside this Bible look brand-new! Have you used the Bible much?"

"Pastor, I use it all the time," she said. "It's just that I can't read. But I carry the Bible with me wherever I go."

A dozen thoughts passed through my mind, none of which would have made my mother proud. *What good is a Bible if you can't read it? The Bible isn't a book of magic – you're not supposed to carry it around like a good luck charm. Maybe we could teach her to read – or maybe not. She's very old. Maybe we could get her granddaughter to read the Bible to her.*

But wouldn't her granddaughter already be doing that, if she could read? I can't remember now exactly what I said, but it wasn't worth remembering.

Does the Bible do any good if you don't read it? I think most of us would say, "No!" The Bible is God's way of communicating to us, and it is our way of getting to know Him. It's meant to be read. What good is a Bible if you don't read it? No good at all, we would say.

But Ana might have given a different answer to that question, if I had bothered to ask her. Even though Ana could not read, she knew what was in that book. The Bible contains the treasures of God – promises of His power and presence, stories of the saints of old, words of comfort for the afflicted, strength for the weak, hope for the hopeless, forgiveness and peace. Grace. Love. If she could not read it, she could at least carry it. For old Ana, the message it contains was as fresh and new as the pages I found in her well-worn Bible. Like an engagement ring on the finger of a bride-to-be, Ana's Bible was a reminder that she was special, chosen, and loved. It was her promise from God. It was her testimony.

Maybe that's why Jesus told the formerly-para-lyzed man to carry his pallet. Because of his healing, that pallet was no longer a bed of bad memories. It had now become a reminder of the love and power of a God who loves the unlovable, and who touches the untouchable. The pallet was his treasure, his testimony. People might ask him, "Why are you carrying your bed?" (People don't usually carry their beds on the street, you know – not even in New Testament times!) And the man might say, "For 38 years this bed carried me. But today, something happened. Today I met Jesus, and now I'm carrying my bed!"

As Christians, we have been touched by God, loved by Him who loves the unlovable. He lifts us from the dust and sets us on our feet. The Word of Life places into our hands His Living Word, the Bible, and tells us to rise and walk. And walk we do – yet so often, we walk away empty-handed. The Bible sits on our shelf, or on the nightstand, or on a pedestal, or in a box, or under the chair. The treasure remains between its covers, undiscovered, left for someone who "has the time" or who "can understand it" or who "is into that kind of thing." And we wonder why our faith never seems to get any stronger, why no one asks us about what we believe. We met Jesus, but we over-look the pallet.

There's an order to these things. "Rise." "Take up your pallet." "Walk."

Ana got it right. She used her Bible all the time. Check the condition of the cover on yours.

2 Corinthians 12:5-10

I will boast about a man like that, but I will not boast about myself, except about my weaknesses. Even if I should choose to boast, I would not be a fool, because I would be speaking the truth. But I refrain, so no one will think more of me than is warranted by what I do or say, or because of these surpassingly great revelations. Therefore, in order to keep me from becoming conceited, I was given a thorn in my flesh, a messenger of Satan, to torment me. Three times I pleaded with the Lord to take it away from me. But he said to me, "My grace is sufficient for you, for my power is made perfect in weakness." Therefore I will boast all the more gladly about my weaknesses, so that Christ's power may rest on me. That is why, for Christ's sake, I delight in weaknesses, in insults, in hardships, in persecutions, in difficulties. For when I am weak, then I am strong.

When I am Weak

Seeing how God deals with our feelings of inadequacy

Do you ever feel that you don't measure up? That other Christians are more gifted or more inspiring or more enterprising or more pleasing to God? I do. I think we all long to make a difference in the world, but often it seems that others are simply more gifted or more capable than we are. It's easy to feel that in comparison to others, we just don't measure up. Those feelings of inadequacy used to bother me, but they don't so much anymore. God showed me the true strength of weakness.

Tuesday afternoons in El Respiro were challenging for me as a young missionary. El Respiro ("the breath") was pretty much right at the end of the world. You drove south out of the city of Maturín for about 30 miles, across the table-flat *llanos* (plains), until you reached the unmarked road that led to the chicken hatchery. Driving again across the *llanos*, on a nearly-deserted road now, past the hatchery, then past the dirt road that takes you to the small town of

La Morrocoya, to nearly the end of the road. Turn again, on a road not much wider than a trail, and follow it until it ends. This is El Respiro – a settlement of perhaps 50 homes, in the absolute center of nowhere.

Our evangelism program in El Respiro consisted mainly of a Bible study that was held on Ramon's front porch. I never learned exactly why we met there – that's just the way it was. Ramon was perhaps in his late 60's, but his still-black hair made him seem younger. Ramon's house had once been green, but time had worn the paint and stucco off the adobe walls, exposing the reddish mud underneath. He always had several chairs set out, and we would sit there and wait for others to gather. Usually old Soltero was the first to arrive. When I first met him, he was over 80, but he wasn't too sure of his exact age. He lived across the road from Ramon – his house used to be pink.

It was a challenging assignment for several reasons. First of all, it wasn't an easy place to find. El Respiro didn't appear on any maps – not that there were many available to begin with. GPS and Google Earth[TM] weren't even a dream back then. Each time I drove out there, I had to trust that my recollection of where to turn would prove to be accurate, since there are not a lot of landmarks out in the Venezuelan plains.

Second, the participants in the Bible study were born and raised in El Respiro. They did not have much in common with a young white man who spoke a strange-sounding version of Spanish. It was hard to find common ground to make conversation, or even to make an analogy to help illustrate the teachings of the Bible.

And it was hard because the missionary who took turns going to El Respiro with me was a well-seasoned veteran. His Spanish was excellent, and he had gained an amazing breadth of knowledge about life in the *campo* (countryside). He had no trouble relating to the people, and they had no trouble understanding him when he spoke. I was certain that in comparison to him, I did not measure up.

Oftentimes, as I sat on Ramon's porch, I wondered to myself, *What am I doing here?* It was pretty clear to me that I was not being very effective. *Couldn't God do what He wanted to do in El Respiro some other way?* I sighed. When one feels out of place, it can be discouraging. It is much easier for us to focus on our deficiencies, instead of our strengths. And when all we see is our mistakes, we are blind to the good that God is doing through us.

On one particular Tuesday afternoon, after I had been visiting El Respiro for about six months, Ramon, Soltero, and I were waiting for the others to arrive, as was our custom. Valiantly trying to engage in some small talk with this white alien on his porch, Ramon opened a new topic: "You aren't from around here, are you?"

I was happy for the question, because it gave me an opportunity to explain why I was so different. "No, I'm not," I said. "I'm from the United States. It's a different country, very far away."

"Farther than Caracas?" asked Soltero. He had been to Caracas once when he was young, perhaps 50 or 60 years ago. It was the farthest he could imagine.

"Much farther than Caracas," I explained. "It is very different where I come from. Most of the people look like me."

That set them back for a while. They looked at me, then looked at each other, then looked around the village. It seemed to me that they were trying to imagine El Respiro populated by tall white men. It was quiet on the porch. Leaves rustled in the breeze.

"What else is different?" Ramon finally asked.

That one set *me* back. Where do I begin? Do I start with the vegetation – how in Michigan there are no palm trees or 8-foot-high grasses? Do I discuss the lack of livestock in the roads, or that people use cars for transportation instead of horses? Do I talk about the weather, the four seasons, and snow? Should I explain that we heat food in a microwave instead of over a wood fire? Or that we have machines that automatically wash our clothes?

Casting about for some point of reference, I noticed a burro plodding along the road, pulling a wooden cart piled high with recently-cut sugarcane. "There are not many burros in the United States," I said. "In fact, where I live, you don't see them at all. And not many carts, either. And the roads are mostly paved and hard, instead of dirt."

They looked at each other. Soltero nodded sagely, remembering his long-ago visit to the big city. "I saw that in Caracas," he said.

I continued. "We don't have sugarcane where I come from. I first learned about sugarcane here, in Venezuela."

That stunned them. Even Caracas has sugarcane! They both fell silent, and for a time it seemed that the conversation was over. Then Ramon said, "You have had to learn a lot of new things!" I nodded in agreement.

Slowly, Soltero got to his feet. He straightened up and took a deep breath, assuming the role of a teacher. "We can help you," he said. "Help you learn." Pointing to a dog lying on the porch, Soltero looked at me and slowly, deliberately, explained: "This is a dog," he said. "Dog."

"Thank you," I said. "We have dogs in the United States."

Soltero exhaled and sat down again. I guess there wasn't much left to say about my strange country that has dogs but no sugarcane. But there was plenty left for me to learn about Venezuela, and about El Respiro, and about the people God had called me to minister to.

What is it that makes us feel inadequate? Is it that we don't know what we are doing? Are we afraid that we will mess up, and that others will notice our deficiencies? It's all of that and more, I think. Deep down, we have this idea that good things happen because somebody who is skilled at it makes it happen. It makes sense to us – the person who is most qualified should be the one to carry it out. If we don't see ourselves as qualified, then it seems clear that we should not be the one doing it – whatever "it" is. We feel most comfortable working within our areas of personal strength. Anything less than that, and we feel inadequate, exposed. And when we do not feel competent, it is hard for us to see how anything worthwhile can come out of what we are doing.

The apostle Paul learned that God works the opposite way – and that strength is actually found in weakness.

> **I was given a thorn in my flesh, a messenger of Satan, to torment me. Three times I pleaded with the Lord to take it away from me. But he said to me, "My grace is sufficient for you, for my power is made perfect in weakness." Therefore I will boast all the more gladly about my weaknesses, so that Christ's power may rest on me. That is**

**why, for Christ's sake, I delight in weak-
nesses, in insults, in hardships, in persecutions, in difficulties. For when I am weak,
then I am strong.** (2 Corinthians 12:7-9)

Paul found that he was most effective in his
weakness because that is when he was most
depending on the power of Christ. In El Respiro, I was
very aware that I was serving in weakness, so in
retrospect I am not surprised that God was at work in
spite of me. What *does* surprise me is the change that
God worked within me. In my weakness, I had no
choice but to depend on the power of Jesus working
through His Spirit. As a result, I grew less reliant on
my own strengths, and more reliant on prayer. I
became less impatient, and more willing to leave the
results in God's hands. I grew less eager to compare
myself with others in a misguided attempt to see my
own success, and more eager to see what the Spirit of
God was doing in the lives of others. I found myself
less concerned with predicting outcomes, and more
concerned with simply taking a first step – content to
wait and see where it would lead. In other words, I
became comfortable ministering in weakness.

About two years later, I returned to Venezuela after my first furlough back in the States. We had been gone for two months, and I was looking forward to getting back into my routine, which included El Respiro on Tuesdays. After Bible study, Soltero walked with me to my car. "What happened to the other missionary?" he asked. It was a fairly common question. Over the years, a good number of missionaries had served in the area. "Which one do you mean?" I wanted to know. "The one who couldn't speak any Spanish," he said, with the typical Venezuelan penchant for exaggeration. I asked for more details about the missionary, trying to figure out who he was referring to. One was very tall and drove a Jeep. Nope. Another was shorter, Brazilian, and had a thin beard. Not him. It couldn't be my El Respiro partner – his Spanish was excellent. I was left with only one conclusion – Soltero was talking about me!

"That was me!" I finally said.

"No," said Soltero. "We understand you fine, and we couldn't understand a word of what the other missionary said!" But I knew that he was referring to me – and that they had been hard-pressed to understand me when I first started in El Respiro.

"No," I said, "it definitely was me. My Spanish got better. You helped me!"

But Soltero was insistent. "If you ever see the other missionary, tell him we said 'hi.'"

I continued going to El Respiro on Tuesdays for another couple of years. Ramon and Soltero eventually decided to make public proclamation of their faith through adult confirmation – perhaps the oldest confirmands in the history of the Lutheran Church of Venezuela. They asked me to officiate at the service which was held one Sunday afternoon in the "big church" in La Morrocoya. In a place where "church" was seen as something for women and children only, the public testimony of two men made quite an impact on the community. Some of the other men in El Respiro ridiculed them, but Ramon and Soltero were not deterred. Standing together, they received our Lord's body and blood in Holy Communion for the first time. Both wore their finest clothes, and Soltero wore his best white cowboy hat.

And if I ever see that other missionary again, I will tell him that Soltero and Ramon said "hi." But I doubt I will ever see him, because that missionary is long gone. In weakness, I was remade by the power of the Spirit into someone I never thought I could be.

For when I am weak, then I am strong.

John 9:1-7

As he went along, he saw a man blind from birth. His disciples asked him, "Rabbi, who sinned, this man or his parents, that he was born blind?"

"Neither this man nor his parents sinned," said Jesus, "but this happened so that the works of God might be displayed in him. As long as it is day, we must do the works of him who sent me. Night is coming, when no one can work. While I am in the world, I am the light of the world."

After saying this, he spit on the ground, made some mud with the saliva, and put it on the man's eyes. "Go," he told him, "wash in the Pool of Siloam" (this word means "Sent"). So the man went and washed, and came home seeing.

Also read John 9:24-38

An Introduction to Hope

Seeing what it really means to share Jesus with others

What do you say to someone who has suffered unspeakable loss? At one time or another, all of us will have to deal with the death of a loved one, which is one of the most trying things that we will face in this life. Death is always difficult, but some situations are especially hard to bear – the senseless tragedy that ends the life of a teenager; or the parent who dies, leaving young children and a heartbroken spouse; or especially, the death of a child. No parent should have to bury their child. For Christians, we know that although death is the end of life on this earth, it is not the end of hope, and hope is what sustains us. On the other hand, what of those who have no hope?

Mariela's mother was a woman without hope. I met Mariela when she started attending the youth group meetings on Saturday evenings at our church in Maturín. She was typical of many of the youth – energetic, full of promise, and looking for something more in life. Mariela's family did not attend our church, or any other, for that matter. Mariela was on her own in that regard, but it seemed that she was finding what she had been looking for. She came regularly, and always with a smile on her face – except for that one Saturday.

The youth were doing what they always do – goofing around, laughing, playing, singing, and getting ready for their meeting. I noticed that Mariela was off by herself, head hanging down. As I approached her to see what was wrong, I could see that she was crying.

"What's the matter?" I asked.

"My brother died," she replied, without looking up.

As a young pastor, I didn't have much experience ministering to the bereaved. In addition, death is handled differently in different cultures, and I had been told that Venezuelans had some specific customs to be followed when there was a death in the family. Looking around, I hoped that some of the other youth would come by and show me the kinds of things that I should say or do, but no one seemed to notice us.

"I'm so sorry," I said, placing my hand on her shoulder. "When did this happen?"

"Last week," she said. This was shocking news to me, because by Venezuelan law the dead had to be buried within 48 hours. If he died last week, that meant the funeral had already happened – and no one from the church had known about it.

"Was he an older brother?" I asked. As a part of our evangelism efforts, I had visited Mariela's family. They lived in a tiny cement house in one of the crowded *barrios* not too far from the church. I had spent a pleasant afternoon with Mariela and her mother, who was a single mother. A brother was not in evidence. Usually in Venezuela, when the pastor comes over to the house to visit (and a foreigner at that!), the whole family is summoned. However, there was always the chance that Mariela had an older brother who was already married and living elsewhere on his own.

"No," she answered. "He was younger."

Since the brother was younger and I had not met him when I visited the home, and since Mariela had never mentioned him before, I was certain that he must have been living in another home, perhaps with a relative. That sometimes happened when a mother could not afford to raise all of her children. "Let's go to where he lived," I suggested, "so I can be with the family, and pray with all of you, and read a little from the Bible."

"No, pastor," she said. "I want to be here now with the youth and take my mind off of things. We can go later – maybe tomorrow."

"Okay," I agreed. "I will go tomorrow after church. Where did he live?"

"At home," she replied, "with us."

I was stunned. "Why didn't I ever meet him?" I finally asked.

She hesitated for a moment, and then looked up at me with a great sadness in her eyes. "Pastor," she explained, "he had... problems. He was disabled." And with that, she started to cry again. I gave her a hug, hoping that my body language would communicate what I could not adequately express with my limited command of Spanish and of Venezuelan culture.

After her sobbing subsided, Mariela explained that her brother was born with severe cerebral palsy. He was essentially a paraplegic, unable to use any of his limbs. He could not walk, talk, sit up, feed himself, or even roll over. Out of shame and embarrassment, his mother kept him in a back bedroom of the house with the curtains drawn and the door closed. When I had visited the family, the brother had been in his crib, not more than 15 feet away from where we sat in the living room.

Theologically, we don't quite know what to make of people who are born with severe disabilities. It doesn't fit well with our idea of a Good and Loving God. But it's not a new question. In fact, when Jesus and his disciples met a man who was blind from birth, the first thing the disciples wanted to know was, ***"who sinned, this man or his parents, that he was born blind?"*** (John 9:2). Afflictions that happen later in life – such as those resulting from accidents or disease – are easier for us to explain. However, if one is born that way, the disciples figured that it must be due to someone's sin. It was a common assumption in New Testament times, and some people still think that way, even today. But Jesus explained, ***"Neither this man nor his parents sinned ... but this happened so that the works of God might be displayed in him."*** (verse 3)

So that the works of God might be displayed in him. Those words echoed in my mind as I went to

Mariela's house the next day. It was not a visit that I was looking forward to making. Children are the pride and joy of all Venezuelans, and a mother's love is legendary. There is really nothing you can say to console a mother upon the death of her child. I also knew that Mariela's mother was sure to have questions similar to the disciples: "Why was my son born like this?" I had serious doubts that telling her that her only son had been born with a severe disability "so that the work of God might be displayed in him" would be either convincing or comforting.

The family – Mariela and her mother, Carmen – were waiting for me when I arrived at their home the next afternoon. Understandably, Carmen was disconsolate. Again and again, she wiped tears from her eyes as I read some Scripture, shared the Gospel, and prayed with her. I tried to get her to talk a little bit about her son, to share her grief. Finally, she spoke.

"I just don't understand..." *Here it comes*, I thought. "... why God would send my son to hell."

Send her son to hell? Where did that come from? And worse yet – what if it's true? Without knowing whether or not her son had faith in Christ, I had carefully avoided discussing the topics of heaven and hell with Carmen. My emphasis was on sharing the love of God with her and Mariela, so that they would trust in Jesus for their own salvation. Especially in this situation, I had wanted to avoid making any kind of pronouncement about whether the son was in heaven or hell. But now, Carmen's question forced the issue.

"Carmen," I asked, "why do you think your son is in hell?"

Mariela then explained that on the previous day, some "evangelicals" from the neighborhood had visited the family. Mariela's mother had raised the topic of heaven, looking for some consolation in the thought that her son was in heaven now, free of his infirmities. But the visitors had quoted Romans 10:9-10:

> **If you declare with your mouth, "Jesus is Lord," and believe in your heart that God raised him from the dead, you will be saved. For it is with your heart that you believe and are justified, and it is with your mouth that you profess your faith and are saved.**

According to their interpretation, since the child was never able to speak, he could not be saved – and was therefore in hell.

This was definitely a time in my ministry when I stopped to thank God that I am a Lutheran. We believe that God works faith through His Word, without any activity on our part. Mute people can have faith. So can the mentally and physically disabled. So can infants, as God applies His word to their soul through the waters of baptism.

"Did you ever take your child to church?" I asked her.

"No," she answered, "it was too hard to put him on the bus. But we sometimes brought him out on the porch at night, so he could feel the cool night air."

"Was he ever baptized?" I asked.

"No, he never went to church," Carmen responded, giving me a look that said, *didn't you just ask that?* Most Venezuelans believe that a baptism can only happen within a church building.

"But what about the *rezaderos*?" I asked. *Rezaderos* are sort of like lay ministers for hire. They learn how to conduct prayers, funeral wakes, and baptisms, and they will come to your house and perform a ceremony or say a prayer, for a price. Sometimes they mix both Christian and non-Christian customs together in a hybrid ceremony. The people do not consider them to be "official church," but in a pinch they will do. Most people believed that a baptism performed by a *rezadero* is just a stopgap measure until the child can be brought to the church for an official baptism by a priest. Among the Lutheran pastors and missionaries, there was an ongoing debate as to whether the custom of *echar el agua* could be considered a valid baptism.

"Oh yes, we had the *rezadero echar el agua* (sprinkle the water) right after my son was born, before we knew what was wrong with him. He did it right here in our living room."

I had no way of knowing exactly what the *rezaderos* had said and done when they "sprinked the water" on the boy, no way to determine whether or not the baptism was done in accordance with the Bible. But Carmen and Mariela were there when it had happened. What they perhaps needed to know was what the Bible teaches about baptism. I told them that baptism does not need to happen in a church because it is God Himself who is at work. I read to her

1 Peter 3:21 (NASB), *"baptism now saves you,"* and also Mark 16:16, *"Whoever believes and is baptized will be saved,"* and other verses on baptism. I explained that Christian baptism is God working the miracle of faith through His Word, which is carried by the water. Similar to the way that Jesus used mud and water to heal the blind man, so also God uses the baptismal waters. Just like the paper and ink of the printed Word are vehicles for the Gospel, so also the water of baptism bears God's saving grace. With many other examples, I shared with them the surprising grace of our God who loved us enough to die for us and offers us forgiveness through such ordinary means.

Sometimes God grants me the privilege of witnessing the conversion of a person as they come to faith in Christ – and when it happens, it is one of the greatest joys of ministry. I am not sure if Mariela's mother was converted at that moment, but at the very least, I got to witness the birth of hope. As I spoke the words of Scripture, Carmen lifted her head. The tears dried from her eyes. A small smile began to form at the corners of her mouth, and the lines of anguish on her face softened and faded. She sat stone still, watching me and listening intently to my every word. Her eyes slowly grew wider, and as I looked into them, for the first time, I saw hope.

When I finished, I turned to Carmen and asked, "Now that you understand a little more about baptism, where do you think your son is right now?"

"My son is in heaven!" she exclaimed. She grasped my hand in hers and drew me closer. "Thank you!" she said. "I knew he was in heaven!"

Is he in heaven? No one wants to condemn the death of an innocent, yet sin condemns us all. Without the intervention of God's grace in Christ, *no one* would be in heaven. After Jesus healed the blind man, the Pharisees were incensed. They questioned the man who was born blind, demanding that he explain how he had been healed – and to give them an answer that did not involve Jesus. The Pharisees strongly believed that Jesus could not heal a blind man. It did not fit their understanding of God. But the healed man would not capitulate. He knew what the rest of us are often slow to learn: The answer *always* involves Jesus. Without Him, there truly is no hope.

In frustration, the Pharisees finally kicked the man out of the temple. Knowing what had happened, Jesus sought him out. When for the first time the man saw the One who had healed him, Jesus asked him the most important question of all:

> **"Do you believe in the Son of Man?"**
>
> **"Who is he, sir?" the man asked. "Tell me so that I may believe in him."**
>
> **Jesus said, "You have now seen him; in fact, he is the one speaking with you."**
>
> **Then the man said, "Lord, I believe,"** **and he worshiped him.** (John 9:35-38)

I can imagine a similar conversation taking place between Jesus and a little boy who never saw Him in church, but was also washed – not in the pool of Siloam, but in his living room.

When our hour has ended, when our lives have been lived, and when the things we will do have been done and the things we regret have been forgotten and nothing is left but memories of love and sorrow, there is only one hope. Jesus.

No Jesus, no hope.

When you introduce someone to Jesus, you intro-duce them to Hope. Once we understand that, it changes the way we think about sharing the Gospel. We're not trying to convince people to believe something they would rather not believe. We are introducing them to Hope.

Hebrews 4:12-16

For the word of God is alive and active. Sharper than any double-edged sword, it penetrates even to dividing soul and spirit, joints and marrow; it judges the thoughts and attitudes of the heart. Nothing in all creation is hidden from God's sight. Everything is uncovered and laid bare before the eyes of him to whom we must give account.

Therefore, since we have a great high priest who has ascended into heaven, Jesus the Son of God, let us hold firmly to the faith we profess. For we do not have a high priest who is unable to empathize with our weaknesses, but we have one who has been tempted in every way, just as we are – yet he did not sin. Let us then approach God's throne of grace with confidence, so that we may receive mercy and find grace to help us in our time of need.

Losing Your Mind

Seeing the difference the Bible makes in our lives

Naked people make me nervous. Not normal naked people in normal situations, like taking a shower or changing clothes. I'm talking about people who go out in public, naked. In Venezuela, I had the experience of encountering a naked person walking down the street a surprising number of times – and it's unsettling. Even in the balmy cities of Venezuela, where the thermometer rarely drops below 75 degrees, clothing is not generally considered optional. So when you see a naked person walking down the street, you probably aren't thinking, *that poor person can't afford clothes*. You think, *crazy*. A naked person in public indicates a certain mental disconnection from reality. It makes you wonder, *if they took off all their clothes, what else might they do?* Naked people on the street seem scary and unpredictable to me.

Not every reality-challenged person in urban Venezuela runs around naked, of course. Most of them wear clothing, sometimes in surprising combinations. If there is a common thread among such people wandering the streets, it is not their clothing (or lack of it). It is the fact that most of them seem to have a Bible among their possessions. Why so many of them have a Bible, I do not know, but that's the way it is.

This detail was brought to my attention one Sunday after church in Maturín. We were in the second week of a monthlong emphasis on the importance of studying the Bible. Our objective was to engage the members in regular weekly Bible study, either at the church or in home study groups. That Sunday, I preached a sermon which clearly linked every possible problem facing the Christian church to a lack of Bible study. By the end, I was expecting the members to fall over themselves in their rush to enroll in the study group of their choice.

After worship, as the members were chatting and eating mangoes outside of the church, a young mother from the congregation came up to me. I was eager to see which Bible study she was planning to attend. (She would have been the first to sign up.)

"Pastor," she said, "reading the Bible will make you crazy."

Okay – that was definitely *not* what I was expecting.

"Why would you say that?" I asked.

"Have you ever seen the crazy people walking around downtown?" she asked. "They are all dirty, they smell bad, they say things that no one can understand, and every one of them has a Bible in their hands. If you want to end up dirty and naked like the crazy people, then go ahead and read the Bible. But if you want to keep your sanity, then stay away from that book!"

How does one respond to that? Clearly, she was afraid of the Bible. That seems so wrong, yet it causes me to wonder: Are *we* afraid of the Bible? Maybe we should be. After all, according to Hebrews,

... the word of God is alive and active. Sharper than any double-edged sword, it penetrates even to dividing soul and spirit, joints and marrow; it judges the thoughts and attitudes of the heart. (Hebrews 4:12)

There is power in the Word. It is able to penetrate to the very inmost depths of our being. It uncovers our secret thoughts and fears. ***"Nothing in all creation is hidden from God's sight. Everything is uncovered*** *and laid bare before the eyes of him to whom we must give account."* (verse 13) The Word of God works on us in ways that we don't fully understand. When we read the Word, it changes us in ways that we can't fully predict or control.

Maybe we already know this about the Bible. Maybe we are afraid of it, and that's why we don't read it in the way that we should. We read it in small doses, in fits and starts, in controllable portions. We are probably not worried about going crazy, but I think we are afraid of *something* – afraid that we will not understand, or that it will be too boring, or that we might find out something about ourselves that we would rather not know. Some might be afraid that they will turn into a "Jesus Freak" – quoting Bible verses all the time, dressing in frumpy clothing, and praying out loud at awkward moments. Are we afraid of what the Bible might do to us?

I have been greatly encouraged to read the Bible not only by my own experience with it, but also by a chapter in Halley's Bible Handbook. This book was one of the first Bible study tools that I ever owned, and it is still on my desk today. It is a curious little book, full of details about the Bible – chapter summaries, archeological notes, maps, and devotional thoughts from the author. One chapter, near the end, is called "The Habit of Bible Reading." Let me give you a taste of Halley's writing style:

> Everybody ought to Love the Bible. Everybody ought to Read the Bible. Everybody. It is God's Word. It holds the Solution of Life. It tells about the Best Friend mankind ever had, the Noblest, Kindest, Truest Man that ever trod this earth.
>
> It is the Most Beautiful Story ever told. It is the Best Guide to human conduct ever known. It gives a Meaning, and a Glow, and a Joy, and a Victory, and a Destiny, and a Glory, to Life elsewhere unknown...
>
> How can any thoughtful person keep his heart from warming up to Christ, and to the Book that tells about Him? Everybody ought to love the Bible. Everybody. EVERYBODY.[3]

---

[3] Halley, Henry H. *Halley's Bible Handbook: An Abbreviated Bible Commentary*. Grand Rapids: Zondervan, 1965. 805.

But the reality is that *not* everyone loves the Bible. Among those who say they do love the Bible, not everyone reads it. And even among those of us who read the Bible, many of us don't read it as regularly as we would like to, or as thoughtfully, or as carefully, or as prayerfully.

Halley's argument is convicting:

> Yet the Widespread Neglect of the Bible by churches and by church people is just simply appalling. Oh, we talk about the Bible, and defend the Bible, and praise the Bible, and exalt the Bible. Yes indeed! But many church members Seldom Ever Even Look Into a Bible...

> We are intelligent about everything else in the world. Why not be intelligent about our religion? We read newspapers, magazines, novels, and all kinds of books, and listen to the radio by the hour. Yet most of us do not even know the names of the Bible books.[4]

---

[4] *Halley's Bible Handbook*, 805 – 806.

Why don't we read the Bible like we should? The reason given to me in Maturín has to be among the most bizarre that I have ever heard, but still, as a pastor, I found it to be surprisingly refreshing. For this one woman, at least, I knew why she was not reading her Bible. She was afraid that the Bible would somehow scramble her brain, and she would end up naked, dirty, and babbling like a lunatic. She was afraid of going crazy.

Yet the fact is that Christians *are* often viewed as "crazy" by those who do not yet know Jesus. The world watches, observing us like we are some aberration of nature that needs to be examined with caution. They simply don't "get" us. We have a different way of understanding ourselves and others. We are guided by different priorities. We live our lives by different standards. We have different morals, different values, different ideas of what is right and wrong. So after due observation, the world concludes that we are nuts.

We object to that conclusion, but there might be something to it, and here's why. If you read your Bible, then I can guarantee that you *will* lose your mind – a mind that God never intended for you to have – the finite, sinful, self-centered mind. In its place, God will give you the mind of Christ. The mind of Christ is one that is governed by God's priorities. It seeks to find the best in others instead of finding fault, to forgive instead of holding grudges, and to love even those who seem unlovable. The mind of Christ soars above the limitations of our human frailty, above the depressing pessimism of the philosophy that "life is all there is, and then you die," and resides in the sweeping story of God's redemption in Christ. The mind of Christ finds purpose and meaning in knowing that we are important and well-thought-out parts of a Master plan, instead of being gloomy, random life forms heading to an inevitable, lemming-like drop into the oblivion of death.

No wonder the world doesn't get us!

The Bible is not dead words on a page. It is a living Word, active, penetrating, insightful. It gives us the mind of Christ, and that changes everything – our way of thinking about ourselves and others, the words we choose to use and avoid, the things we decide to do and not do, our motivations, goals, and ambitions, our relationships, our self-image. *Everything*.

And if that's what people call "crazy," then mark me down for two cases of nuts.

Turns out that my friend in Maturín was not so far off the mark, after all.

Matthew 17:14-20

When they came to the crowd, a man approached Jesus and knelt before him. "Lord, have mercy on my son," he said. "He has seizures and is suffering greatly. He often falls into the fire or into the water. I brought him to your disciples, but they could not heal him."

"You unbelieving and perverse generation," Jesus replied, "how long shall I stay with you? How long shall I put up with you? Bring the boy here to me." Jesus rebuked the demon, and it came out of the boy, and he was healed at that moment.

Then the disciples came to Jesus in private and asked, "Why couldn't we drive it out?"

He replied, "Because you have so little faith. Truly I tell you, if you have faith as small as a mustard seed, you can say to this mountain, 'Move from here to there,' and it will move. Nothing will be impossible for you."

Powerful Prayer

Seeing what happens when we pray

Do you ever question the power of prayer? I do. I admire those people who are "prayer warriors," who pray fervently and faithfully and never seem to have any doubt about the effectiveness of their prayers. I admire them because I am not one of them. I pray, but I also have questions about how this whole "prayer thing" really works. I find myself wondering: *What's the point? After all, doesn't God know everything? Doesn't He already know what I think and feel, and what I need, even better than I do?* Perhaps you have asked yourself the same kinds of questions. I think the problem is that prayer does not seem to fit well with our idea of God. Prayer seems... redundant. Sure, we understand all the "right" reasons for prayer: prayer is a conversation; it is building our relationship with God; it is for our benefit, not for God's. But the idea that God might withhold His blessings until we ask for them in the prescribed way diminishes God by making Him into some kind of capricious Santa, instead of honoring Him as our sovereign Lord.

As a missionary, I found that people had high expectations for the effectiveness of my prayers. (And by "effective," they mean getting a desired result.) In Venezuela, most things in society operate on the principle of *palanca. Palanca* means influence, weight, or pull. People with *palanca* are those who have high positions in government or in business; they are the ones who can get you a job, solve a problem for you, or make things happen. Everyone thought that since I am a pastor, I have *palanca* with God. It made perfect sense to them. And although I might wish that it were true, the reality is that my prayers are no more effective than theirs, or yours, or anyone else's in producing a specific result. Even those in full-time ministry don't always get what they pray for.

The disciples certainly found this out in Matthew 17:14-20. A man brought his son to Jesus for healing because the son was suffering from convulsions and seizures caused by a demon. This was not the first time the father had sought help for his boy. He had already brought him to the disciples, but they had been unable to do anything. (***"I brought him to your***

disciples, but they could not heal him." (verse 16))
Clearly, the father went to the disciples because he
believed their prayers would be more effective than
his own. But it didn't turn out that way. In this case,
the prayers of the disciples did not yield the result the
man had wanted. They, too, were familiar with the
same feelings of frustration and discouragement that
we struggle with ourselves. Why are some prayers
answered right away, while others seem to fall on deaf
ears? What is the power of prayer?

Ramona came into our church in Barquisimeto
one Sunday morning near the end of the service, her
toddler daughter in tow. When Ramona entered, I was
sure that she was homeless and living in the street –
tangled hair, stained and dirty clothing, and with the
aroma of one who has been too long without a bath.
Yet beneath all of that, one could see that in better
times, Ramona was strikingly beautiful. Now, however, she was quite obviously distraught. As we tried
to talk to her, she began weeping and wailing as only
a Venezuelan woman can – long moans, heartrending
sobs, copious tears. She was the picture of suffering.

Members of the congregation stayed by her side as she continued to wail all through the Bible study hour. We consoled her and prayed with her, and little by little her story came out. She was a single mother, unemployed, with three children – two sons, and the toddler daughter who was with her. Her oldest son was in a detention facility. The immediate concern was her middle son, 11 years old, who had run away from home and had been missing for nearly a month. Ramona had exhausted her meager resources searching for him, and now she was completely destitute. She told us that she had gone to several churches seeking help. Like the man with the suffering son in Matthew 17, Ramona was desperate. So far, no one had been able to help. But she held onto that tiny seed of hope that maybe this time would be different.

When the man brought his demon-possessed son to Jesus, Jesus healed him. Just like that! But before doing so, He gave us a hint in verse 17 as to why others had not been able to do the same: ***"You unbelieving and perverse generation"***! And later, when the disciples asked why they had not been able to heal the boy, Jesus explained,

Because you have so little faith. Truly I tell you, if you have faith as small as a mustard seed, you can say to this mountain, "Move from here to there," and it will move. Nothing will be impossible for you. (verse 20)

I'll be the first to admit it: If all it takes is faith the size of a tiny mustard seed to move a mountain, then I have little faith. Maybe you feel the same way. Oh, we believe that God could move a mountain, no doubt about it. I believe that He could with all my heart! What I struggle with is that He *would*. I tend to think, "Why would God move a mountain into the sea?" So I have never asked Him to. In prayer, I find that I often "hedge my bets" by only asking God to do what I can imagine Him actually doing. At some level, I suppose I am trying to help God along so that His answer will more often coincide with my desired outcome, which would make my prayers seem more effective.

Ramona was probably hoping that my prayers, and the prayers of our church, would somehow be "better" than hers, more "effective" at moving her mountain. She wanted us to pray for the impossible – that in a city of over 1 million people, God would help her find her son who clearly did not want to be found. She believed we had *palanca*, but I knew better. The God that we serve is a God who hears our prayers and cares deeply about our concerns, more deeply than we will ever know. He doesn't need to be approached by someone with *palanca* before He will listen, so I prayed for God to help Ramona find her son. We all did. But if truth be told, I really wasn't expecting much on this one. I was pretty sure that this was not a prayer that God would answer the way Ramona wanted it to be answered.

In the city of Barquisimeto, we had a ministry contact office that was located some distance from the property that we rented for worship services. Ramona had come to us at the worship location. A few days later, a family came to the ministry contact office – it was their first time coming to us. They had been housing a young boy whom they had found on the street. They were hoping that he would go back to his home, but he was reluctant to leave. Finally, the family decided that they needed to do something. They saw "Christ" on our ministry office sign, and figured maybe this would be the place to bring him. Unbelievably, it was Ramona's son!

This whole event reminds me of the story of Jesus' encounter with the widow of Nain in Luke 7:11-17. As Jesus was entering the village with His disciples, they met a group heading out to the cemetery. A widow, weeping and wailing, was going to bury her only son. This was the end of her world, because according to Jewish law, widows were not allowed to own property. They either had to remarry or their sons had to provide for them. So not only had this woman lost her beloved son, but she also lost all her property, her income, and her retirement! She had every reason to cry.

In that context, the counsel that Jesus gave to the widow sounds impossible. He said, ***"Don't cry"*** (verse 13). We said something similar to Ramona, too, when she first came to us. But the increasing volume of Ramona's wails gave us her response: *You don't understand my pain, my anguish, the depth of my despair. You are asking the impossible. There is nothing left for me to do but weep.*

Why would Jesus tell the heartbroken, "Don't cry?" He knew all about the widow's grief, just as He knew all about Ramona's problems. He knows why we cry, why we are weighed down with hurt and despair. He knows the losses we suffer, the pain we experience, and the disappointments that knock us down and drive hope from our souls. He knows all of that. When Jesus said, "Don't cry," He was not referring to the past. He was saying it in anticipation of what was coming!

> **"Young man, I say to you, get up!" The dead man sat up and began to talk, and Jesus gave him back to his mother.** (verses 14-15)

We, too, gave the young man back to his mother. I know the joy that the woman of Nain felt upon receiving her son because I saw it on Ramona's face. Tears, copious again, streamed down – but this time they were tears of joy, wetting both her face and her son's as she kissed him again and again. "Thank you, thank you, thank you!" Ramona said to us, over and over and over again. As we watched that blessed reunion with tears in our own eyes, it was clear that we had witnessed a miracle – at least for Ramona, even if her son might not have agreed. We all knew that we had done nothing to find her son – absolutely nothing – except pray. God had worked this one out, all by Himself. The mountain moved!

Why did *this* mountain move, while others didn't? What am I missing, here? Were our prayers for Ramona somehow different than all of the other prayers that we had prayed in the past? Did we pray with more faith? Did we pray more fervently? I don't think so. The reality is that Ramona's mountain was not moved because our prayers were somehow "better" or more effective than other prayers we've made. It is always God who acts. God casts out the demon. God raises the dead to life. God reunites mother and son. God heals, God comforts, God strengthens, God encourages, God forgives. God is the mountain-mover, not our prayer.

Prayer is an invitation for God to act. I have invited a lot of people to different events in my life. When you invite someone, sometimes they say yes, and sometimes they say no. But if you don't invite them, then you are still communicating something to them – you are essentially saying that you would prefer that they not come. When we don't pray, we are saying to God: "I prefer that You not get involved here. You are not invited."

But when we pray – ah, when we pray! – we are opening the door of invitation for God to be who He is. Prayer is not *palanca*. Prayer does not trick God into acting, or coerce Him into acting, or shame Him into acting. Prayer doesn't manipulate Him in any way. It's an invitation.

Ramona's unexpected miracle opened my eyes to see the real power of prayer. Our prayers do not make things happen – when we pray, we are inviting God to do His thing. Sometimes God intervenes in our lives on His own, without our asking, but much of the time He waits for an invitation. And when we invite Him, He always shows up! God never declines an invitation. He may not always show up in the way we want Him to – moving our mountains the way we want them moved, miraculously solving our problems – but He is always present. Sometimes He comes with peace and comfort; sometimes, with strength and courage; sometimes, with hope and a promise.

And sometimes, because we invited Him, He comes with miracles. Now that's powerful prayer!

Luke 15:11-20, and 32

Jesus continued: "There was a man who had two sons. The younger one said to his father, 'Father, give me my share of the estate.' So he divided his property between them.

"Not long after that, the younger son got together all he had, set off for a distant country and there squandered his wealth in wild living. After he had spent everything, there was a severe famine in that whole country, and he began to be in need. So he went and hired himself out to a citizen of that country, who sent him to his fields to feed pigs. He longed to fill his stomach with the pods that the pigs were eating, but no one gave him anything.

"When he came to his senses, he said, 'How many of my father's hired servants have food to spare, and here I am starving to death! I will set out and go back to my father and say to him: Father, I have sinned against heaven and against you. I am no longer worthy to be called your son; make me like one of your hired servants.' So he got up and went to his father.

"But while he was still a long way off, his father saw him and was filled with compassion for him; he ran to his son, threw his arms around him and kissed him. ... 'we had to celebrate and be glad, because this brother of yours was dead and is alive again; he was lost and is found.'"

My Prodigal Son

Seeing how God works in ways we never could have guessed

———————⟡———————

Ever wonder why people do the things that they do? Sometimes the decisions people make, or the actions they take, or the words they say leave me bewildered. *What could they possibly be thinking?*, I wonder. Venezuelans have a saying for this kind of situation: *Cada cabeza es un mundo* – every head is its own world. We may never know or understand why people do the things they do, because their world is not our world, their head is not ours. But still, sometimes it would be nice to know.

That was the case with Ramona's son, Oscar, who ran away from home when he was about 11 years old and took up residence with strangers for a month. His mother had been frantic with worry, exhausting every resource to find him. After God miraculously reunited mother and son (described more fully in the previous chapter, "Powerful Prayer"), Ramona was overjoyed, but Oscar clearly was not. After their reunion,

Ramona and Oscar began to attend our church regularly, and soon both were well integrated into the life of the congregation. However, I often wondered why Oscar ran away, and even though I tried to ask him about it, he was either unable or unwilling to tell me his reasons. I knew that life was hard for the family, living on subsistence wages in a tin shack no larger than a small bedroom. I also knew that Oscar had to shoulder much more responsibility in the home than any 12-year-old kid should, caring for his younger sister and helping his mother deal with the challenges of a life of poverty. Still, there were many other boys in Oscar's situation who would never imagine running away from home or abandoning their family, so I wondered what he was thinking. After my inquiries went nowhere, I had to satisfy myself with the Venezuelan answer: Every head is its own world – *cada cabeza es un mundo*.

The father of the prodigal son in Luke 15 probably also wished that he could understand what his younger son was thinking when he asked for his share of the inheritance and left home. The father was providing everything for his family – food, shelter, a loving environment, servants, and more. It was a life that many people of that time would have envied. Yet when the son decided to leave home, the father did not stand in his way, even though he surely did not understand what the boy was thinking. The father knew his son was making a mistake, but he let it happen.

I sometimes wish that I could help other people avoid mistakes, and sometimes I wish that God would have helped me avoid the big mistakes that I've made in my own life. But God lets it happen, because His goal is that we become stronger, wiser, and more mature Christians – and that usually comes from living through our mistakes, rather than avoiding them. As it turns out, Oscar had to live through quite a few of his mistakes.

Shortly after Oscar's conversion, the congregation purchased some property in the city of Barquisimeto in order to build a permanent church. As a missionary, I invited our supporting congregations back in the United States to send short-term mission teams to Venezuela to help us with the construction. Soon, we were hosting several teams per year. Members of the Barquisimeto congregation would participate in the building with each team from the States, and many friendships were formed. Oscar was a permanent fixture with the teams – eagerly helping out, learning a few words of English, and providing our visitors with a glimpse into the life of a young man who was growing up in a world very different from their own.

Team members inevitably would ask me to tell them about Oscar. They were curious about his story, and wanted to know what they could do to give him a chance at a better future. Eventually, a scholarship fund was established for Oscar to enable him to attend a private Christian academy close to the church. This was a tremendous blessing, because the public schools in Venezuela were a complete disaster. They were overcrowded, understaffed, and poorly equipped, and it was not uncommon for students to miss an entire year of school due to interruptions in funding or administrative incompetence. It seemed clear to everyone that if Oscar was going to have a chance at a better life, he needed a better education. Just as the father of the prodigal son provided abundantly for his family, all those who had been touched by Oscar were determined to provide him with the best possible future.

The fund was established, and the tuition was paid – but Oscar did not do well. Soon, he began skipping classes, and was placed under the school's disciplinary procedures. Ramona was at her wits' end. Even with the support of the congregation, together we were unable to convince Oscar to apply himself in his studies and take advantage of the wonderful opportunity that had been given to him. Finally, Oscar was deemed to be a detriment to the learning environment, and was expelled from the school.

I had a hard time explaining to Oscar's supporters back in the States what had happened. No one, myself included, could believe that this young man who was so helpful, bright, and engaging at church, could be such a poor student at school – surly, uncooperative, disrespectful to his teachers, and a bad influence on his peers. Soon, he was back to the public schools and all the disadvantages of such an environment. Truly, compared to the education that he had forfeited, Oscar was now eating with the swine.

As Oscar grew older, his participation at the church became more sporadic, although his mother Ramona remained as faithful as ever. After my family and I eventually moved away from Venezuela, I kept track of Oscar through occasional updates from Ramona or the other church members. Like the father who stood by the road watching for his son's return, I watched for news of Oscar. I heard that he had run away several more times, that he had been conscripted into the military, that he was now out of the army, and was unemployed and living in Caracas. It seemed that his life was going nowhere. Then one day, out of the blue, he appeared once again, like the prodigal son in the distance, coming down the road toward home. Word came that Oscar was once again back in Barquisimeto and was attending church regularly. He reportedly was a new man! Soon, Oscar enrolled in the Venezuelan theological education program, and his hard work made a good impression on all of his teachers. I was overjoyed with his new direction, but had my doubts as to whether or not he would stick with it. But to my surprise, after two years, Oscar was ready for vicarage. (In Venezuela, vicarage is a two-year pastoral internship.)

What had happened to Oscar? Had God really given him a new heart and mind? I really wanted to know. I had my opportunity to talk with Oscar about it when I was invited back to Venezuela to teach a theology course for pastors and church leaders. Oscar was in the class – his attendance was required as a part of his pastoral training. At one point, we were able to sit down together and talk at length. The story Oscar told me went something like this:

"When I was a boy, life in our home was very hard. My mother was angry all the time, and she would come home and beat us. That's why I ran away that one time, when you found me.

"After she learned about Jesus, we all became Christians, and my mom tried really hard to change. But when I saw your family, I knew that was the family I wanted. I wanted a mom and a dad who loved me and took care of me. I didn't want to have to take care of my mom. When all of the people came from the United States, I imagined that all of their families were like yours. I spent as much time with them at church as I could, because I wanted someone to adopt me and take me to live with them in their perfect family.

"I didn't like school, because it was too much like my home – people telling me what to do, and if I didn't do it, then there were consequences. And I knew that if I did well in school, that would mean I was growing up and didn't need to be adopted. I know

now that I squandered an opportunity of a lifetime, and I can't tell you how sorry I am.

"After I left home, I wandered around a lot, looking for a family. But wherever I went, I kept thinking about my church in Barquisimeto, and I remembered all the people there – until I finally realized that the church *was* my family. Everything that I had been looking for, I already had at my church, but I had thrown it all away – just like the prodigal son. When I realized that, I came back right away. My mom took me in again, and I joined the church again, and everyone was so happy to see me, and I realized that I was home. Now I want to be a pastor just like you, and help everyone who is looking for a family to find it in the family of Christ."

The prodigal son returned. My prodigal son.

~

I would like to add a few final words. I always enjoyed listening to the commentator Paul Harvey on the radio. His segment called *The Rest of the Story* was my favorite. In his inimitable cadence, Harvey would tell a story that celebrated the good of humanity – something heartwarming, or amazing, or ingenious – narrated in a way that enthralled the listener. Then came the best part: the "rest of the story." Without changing his delivery, Harvey would add some other detail that brought an unexpected revelation – for example, that the hero of the story was a well-known historical figure, or perhaps that the story laid the groundwork for an invention or an event that changed history. The rest of the story helped everything that came before it make sense.

The reason God answered Ramona's prayer to find her son is that Oscar needed a family, and the family that he needed was God's family at our church. If Ramona had not come to our church for help in her time of need, if we had not prayed, if her son had not been found, if any of those things had not happened, then Oscar might never have become the man that he is today. To my unending delight, Oscar was ordained as a Lutheran pastor.

Every head is its own world, and God lives in all of them. We often have no idea what God has in mind – what His plans and His purposes are – and how we fit into those plans. We don't understand why some things happen the way they do. But then again, we don't have to. We often think of ourselves as the prodigal son, but in that parable the father is truly a model of what God expects of us. We do our best to help others choose the right path. We accept their decisions, however foolish they might seem. Then we stand by the road, and wait.

And sometimes, we get to see the prodigal son come home.

And now you know the rest of the story.

God's Mission Today

What would it be like if you did not know your own feet? Or if your hands were strangers to you? When we talk about the Church as the "body of Christ," we usually think of our own local congregation. Some members are the hands, some are the feet, some are the eyes, the ears, and all the rest of the parts of the body (cf. 1 Corinthians 12). It is also true, though, that the body of Christ is the whole Christian Church on earth, and that the parts of this body are scattered throughout the nations of the world. The Church in one country might be the hands; in another country, the feet; and so on around the world. A church without the interaction and exchange of cross-cultural mission would be a church that does not know the members of her own body.

Yet sadly, it seems that the Christian Church today in many places is backing away from the sending of missionaries. In some places, "mission" is being redefined as "being a Christian wherever you are," resulting in a loss of enthusiasm for sending people to other nations. In other cases, missionaries are being

called off the field against their will for either financial or "strategic" reasons. In Venezuela, for example,
between 2003 and 2004, denominational mission
officials decided to remove all missionaries from
Venezuela due to "strategic and financial reasons."
The forced withdrawal of the Lutheran missionary
team resulted in incalculable harm to the national
church. Today, the Lutheran Church of Venezuela is a
tiny church body of scarcely 600 members, suffering
from economic deprivations and a lack of trained
leadership at nearly all levels. Compounded by many
societal problems and a challenging political environment, the Lutheran Church of Venezuela needs our
prayers and support now more than ever.

The Cooling of Our Passion for Missions

One might ask, "Why would churches or Christian
organizations ever decide to stop sending missionaries?" One of the reasons is that television, the
Internet, and other forms of mass communication have
made us all more aware of the needs right in our own
communities. This causes some to say, "There are so
many needs right here. We should focus on those
closest to us. Aren't there Christians in those other

countries? Let them take care of their needs, and we will take care of ours." The Church is pictured as something like an island in its own community, rowing out into nearby waters.

The picture that we get from Scripture, though, is quite different. God wants His Church to be a sending Church. Jesus said, *"As the Father has sent me, I am sending you"* (John 20:21), and also, *"go and make disciples of all nations"* (Matthew 28:19). While our own communities have great needs, other communities around the world also have great needs. If Christian workers were distributed around the world on the basis of need, there would be far fewer in the United States and other historically Christian nations, and far more in places like the Middle East, Asia, and North Africa.

Others have pointed out that ministering cross-culturally is expensive and difficult. A foreigner will never master the language or the culture as well as one who is born there. From a financial standpoint, if one is to work in another country, it makes more sense to invest in training national leaders than it does to send cross-cultural missionaries. But before we start training, the question must be asked: Who is qualified to be a trainer of church leaders in that country? The preparation of leaders for Christian ministry is not purely academic. Book learning must be combined with practical application and ministry skills which are appropriate for the specific context. A person who has never lived in that place, who does not speak the language of the people, and who has never ministered under those specific conditions is not well-qualified to teach. A missionary, on the other hand, has one foot in each of two worlds. He or she becomes a type of cultural bridge, allowing skills and knowledge to pass from one culture and context to another.

Re-kindling the Fire

Most compelling to me, though, is the urgent need for Gospel proclamation in the light of our ever-increasing global population. As the number of people on earth increases, so also does the number of those who will die without ever hearing the Good News of forgiveness and salvation in Jesus Christ. Over the past 100 years, the proportion of Christians in the world has actually declined slightly, from about 35%

in 1910 to about 32% in 2010.[5] With a current world population of something over seven billion, this means that there are four to five billion people alive today who do not believe in Jesus.[6]

The exciting news, though, is not found in percentages of Christians, but in their location. While Christianity has been slowly declining in Europe and North America, it has been growing rapidly in Africa, Asia, and Latin America. There has been a monumental shift in the Christian "center of gravity," with the largest and most vital churches now located in what has been called the "Global South." Using my own denomination as an example, the Lutheran Church – Missouri Synod has been declining by about 50,000 souls per year, and now numbers something like 2.3

---

[5] Pew Research Center, March 22, 2013, "Number of Christians Rises, But Their Share of World Population Stays Stable," http://www.pewresearch.org/daily-number/number-of-christians-rises-but-their-share-of-world-population-stays-stable/, accessed January 1, 2014.

[6] The estimate depends on various assumptions. For example, the Pew Study puts the percentage of Christians in Latin America at about 90%. Evangelical Christian groups estimate that only 10% of Latin Americans are Christians. The difference is due to whether or not one includes all nominal Roman Catholics as "Christians."

million. In contrast, the Mekane Yesus Lutheran Church of Ethiopia has over 6 million members, and is growing rapidly. The Lutheran Church of Tanzania is not far behind, with close to 6 million members. In Madagascar, Lutherans are some 3.5 million strong, and plant a new church in their country every day. These churches, and many others like them, are the harvest from the seeds that were planted by cross-cultural missionaries from Europe and North America over the last 200 years.

With that kind of exciting growth, one needs to ask: Where are *their* missionaries? The commission of Jesus to go *"to the ends of the earth"* (Acts 1:8) was given to all Christians, not just to those who live in the "Global North." Take a moment and imagine with me what missions would look like today if Christians from every nation were mobilized as cross-cultural missionaries. Imagine what God could do if the churches of the Global South were to send their sons and daughters into all the world as missionaries, bringing not only the Gospel, but also their vitality, joy, and enthusiasm for Jesus. Imagine if every church on earth were a sending church!

A New Vision – Global Lutheran Outreach

In 2010, God laid on my heart the vision to raise up a missionary force from all the nations of the world. Global Lutheran Outreach is an independent Lutheran mission organization dedicated to sending missionaries "from everywhere to everywhere." Our piece in God's mission is to work with Lutheran churches and individuals around the world so that more and more missionaries are sent, until every Lutheran church is a sending church and every person on earth has heard the Good News of salvation in Jesus!

As a global body of Christ, the possibilities are limitless. When missionaries from every country where the Church has been established contribute to cross-cultural Gospel proclamation with the gifts they have been given, the face of mission will be changed. New ideas and creativity will be brought to bear. Language groups that were once extremely difficult or inaccessible will become accessible. Places that have been closed to Western missionaries will be open to those from other nations. We will see new and creative approaches, reflecting the diversity and uniqueness of each missionary and each sending church. In short, we will see the dawn of a new age of mission.

> **How, then, can they call on the one they have not believed in? And how can they believe in the one of whom they have not heard? And how can they hear without someone preaching to them? And how can anyone preach unless they are sent? As it is written: "How beautiful are the feet of those who bring good news!"** (Romans 10:14-15)

I hope that God has used this book to kindle in your heart a passion for missions! God invites all of us to be a part of His mission to the world. Some are called to pray, some are called to give, and some are called to go. To learn more and to find your place in God's mission, visit our website: www.Global LutheranOutreach.com.

Global Lutheran Outreach
from everywhere to everywhere

Experience the Joy!

Our passion is to help Lutherans experience the joy of participating with God in His mission to reach all nations with the Gospel!

The world is getting a little bit smaller every day. More and more, we are globally engaged through the media, through our jobs, and through our network of relationships. People who love Jesus are asking, "Why can't we do global mission work right from our church?"

The global Lutheran church is getting bigger every day. Lutheran Christians around the world are asking, "Why can't we be missionaries, too?"

YOU CAN! Global Lutheran Outreach finds a way to connect mission passion with mission opportunities. We find a way to say, "YES!"

Here's what we provide:

- **Long-term missionary service:** Long-term missionaries serve for an open-ended period of time, beginning with a two year commitment.

- **Enable non-Western Lutherans to serve as cross-cultural missionaries:** We seek to mobilize the global Lutheran Body of Christ for cross-cultural missionary service.

- **Student Mission Experience:** Lutheran university students in the Student Mission Experience program serve in a cross-cultural overseas setting for six months to two years.

- **Send and support missionaries from your own congregation:** We can help!
  - Locate the "right fit" with an overseas partner
  - Missionary training: pre-field and on-field
  - Facilitate travel documents
  - International currency transfers and medical insurance

Rev. Dr. James Tino, Director
E-mail: director@globallutheranoutreach.com
Website: www.GlobalLutheranOutreach.com

Also from Tri-Pillar Publishing

Life As a Mission Trip

DR. JACOB YOUMANS

Missional Living 101!

Trips to the mission field always bring new spiritual growth and insight to our lives. What if we could learn to see mission not as an event to take part in, but as a lifestyle to embrace? In *Missional U: Life As a Mission Trip*, that's exactly what Dr. Jacob Youmans teaches us as he shows, through Scripture and by personal example, what missional living is all about! If you're looking for a new way to travel, then come along. Missional U is your ticket to an exciting and fulfilling spiritual adventure – one that's sure to last a lifetime!

Dr. Jacob Youmans, a dynamic conference speaker, is Director of the DCE Program at Concordia University in Austin, Texas.

$14.95 – Order online at ww.tripillarpublishing.com

MISSIONAL TOO

The Trip of a Lifetime

Dr. Jacob Youmans

Bon Voyage... Again!

In this second volume of devotions on the joy of missional living, Dr. Jacob Youmans shows us what it means to see the world through redemptive eyes, love the world with an evangelistic heart, and travel the world with the Gospel of peace firmly on our feet. In *Missional Too: The Trip of a Lifetime*, we discover that when we walk in the footsteps of Jesus, the imprint we leave behind is His, not our own – and that makes all the difference. Our journey here as God's dearly loved people is a Gospel-sharing, disciple-making one.

Dr. Jacob Youmans, a dynamic conference speaker, is Director of the DCE Program at Concordia University in Austin, Texas.

$14.95 – Order online at ww.tripillarpublishing.com

Shaking Scripture

Grasping More of God's Word

Rev. Mark Manning

Shaking Scripture was written to help develop a hunger within you for God's Word. You will see how intriguing and interesting the Bible can be. You will be guided through some of the well-known stories we've grown to love and that have, perhaps, gotten stale with familiarity. In addition, you will discover some lesser-known stories that just might surprise you because of their readability and application. In all, there are 12 devotions, each aimed at "Shaking Scripture" in a way that helps us grasp more of God's Word. Several reflective questions per devotion are also provided, making this book ideal for individual or group study.

Rev. Mark Manning serves as Associate Pastor of St. Paul's Lutheran Church in Orange, CA, where he shares his passion for understanding Scripture.

$14.95 – Order online at ww.tripillarpublishing.com

Abba Daddy Do

exploration **s** in child like faith

by Dr. Jacob Youmans

Join the adventure of childlike faith!

When you're a child, every day is an adventure!
Each day you see and experience life for the very
first time. Reclaim the wonder and excitement meant
for followers of Jesus as we explore the gift of
childlike faith. Jacob Youmans, father of two, walks
us through 40 true-life stories, discovering the
spiritual in the everyday moments of childhood.
Complete with study questions and scriptural
references, this book is perfect for the individual
looking to grow and be challenged, as well as a
family or Bible study group.

Dr. Jacob Youmans, a dynamic conference speaker, is Director
of the DCE Program at Concordia University in Austin, Texas.

$14.95 – Order online at ww.tripillarpublishing.com

by Rev. Dr. Lloyd Strelow

You've got questions - God's love provides the answers!

Powerful Love gets to the core of the essence of our Christian faith. The first chapter opens the window to God's love for each of us. It is through that window - guided by the Holy Spirit - that Christians see, believe, and live the rest of God's Word. Throughout Powerful Love, Pastor Strelow uses the inductive method, using our questions to lead us to search God's Word and find His answers for faith and life. Written as a basic guide to the Christian faith, Powerful Love also includes thoughtful study questions and an introductory guide

Rev. Dr. Lloyd Strelow has served six congregations in Michigan and California, including Prince of Peace Lutheran Church (LCMS) in Hemet, CA, where one of his primary emphases was to teach the basics of the Christian faith to all who seek to know the Lord.

$12.95 – Order online at ww.tripillarpublishing.com

tALKING PICTURES

*How to turn a trip to the
movies into a mission trip*

by Dr. Jacob Youmans
Foreword by Leonard Sweet

Movies and ministry? What's the story?

Movies are everywhere - at the theater, at home, on
our computers, even in our pockets! Our culture's
fascination with the power of movies brings us
together in a shared experience. But did you ever
think that watching the latest action-adventure flick
with a friend could provide a truly unique opportunity to witness about your Christian faith? Talking
Pictures examines the power of movies in our culture
and explores effective ways in which we can use any
movie as a way to start conversations about our
Christian faith.

Dr. Jacob Youmans, a dynamic conference speaker, is Director
of the DCE Program at Concordia University in Austin, Texas.

$14.95 – Order online at ww.tripillarpublishing.com

Extraordinary News

for ordinary people

by Rev. Heath Trampe

What's so special about being ordinary?

In a world which equates "ordinary" with "not good enough," Rev. Heath Trampe uses powerful examples from the Bible to prove that even ordinary people can accomplish amazing things. As you journey through these 12 stories of inspiration and hope, you'll discover that "ordinary" is a pretty amazing thing to be. This 214-page book includes Bible study questions for each chapter, with in-depth answers and commentary. It is ideal for both individual and group study.

INDIE 2010 NEXT GENERATION BOOK AWARDS FINALIST!

Reverend Heath Trampe graduated in May 2010 with a Masters of Divinity from Concordia Theological Seminary in Fort Wayne, Indiana. Heath is currently serving as Associate Pastor of St. Peter's Lutheran Church in Fort Wayne.

$14.95 – Order online at ww.tripillarpublishing.com

CPSIA information can be obtained at www.ICGtesting.com
Printed in the USA
LVOW10s0509280514

387564LV00001B/1/P